Wine In T

MW00399072

My Cosmic Adventures through Desert Storm

by

Jim White

Dedication

To my dearest Desert Girl, Mary. Wow, what an adventure it has been!
I'm pretty sure the point of the entire war was to bring us together.

Editor

Julie Dunn Crawford
I wrote an essay, you made it a book.
Thank you.

Cover By

Karen Minzner
WOW!

Prologue

If you have picked this up expecting a history of Operation Shield/Storm, then immediately put this back where you found it. This isn't that. However, if you want a good laugh and the story of one guy's point of view on how he found himself in the middle of a war, you came to the right place.

In August of 1990, in response to Iraq invading Kuwait, George H.W. Bush declared a "LINE IN THE SAND" had been drawn. If Saddam Hussein did not recognize this line, some good 'ole American whoop-ass would soon follow. Saddam did not, and what followed was amazing.

In the middle of that was me. Stuck on a roller coaster of a relationship, only four months left of my enlistment, and already signed up for college next semester, I suddenly found my life upside down. Having grown up watching M*A*S*H, and wielding the DNA of an adventurer, I made some lemonade out of some of the worst lemons life could hand you and jumped headfirst into the greatest escapade of my young life.

What follows is my journey. From sitting on a sandy beach in Florida to filling sandbags in Saudi Arabia, this tells the story of the many twists, turns, and unexpected U-turns in those weird few months of 1990/91. Lessons were learned, and my life was changed forever. I learned to not fight the universe since it always wins in the end. Atlantis! Scream it loud!

Disclaimer

I'm not a writer. Also, I'm not a historian. I'm a guy who had a story to tell and was finally able to type it out. You may very well find some historical errors within the pages that follow. It would be a miracle if you didn't. This is an account of what happened to me, to the best of my recollection. Also, if you are easily offended, then perhaps you shouldn't look further. Lastly, don't get hung up on dates and numbers. I didn't.

Chapter 1
In The Beginning…

Want to know what's scarier than *knowing* you're gonna die in thirty seconds? Knowing that you *might* die in thirty seconds. Imagine you're in a warehouse, tied to a chair, duct tape over your mouth. Sitting across from you is a psychopath with an old six-shooter gun. He holds up one bullet and says, "In thirty seconds, I'm going to kill you." He puts the bullet in the gun, stands up, walks over to you, pulls back the hammer and counts down the seconds. The duct tape over your mouth stops you from even trying to reason with this person. For thirty seconds, you are forced to live through every emotion you've ever had. Regret. Anger. Fear. No last "goodbyes", no last "I love you" or "I'm sorry", just this man counting down the seconds....3. 2. 1. You're doomed.

But what if instead, the guy puts the bullet in the chamber, spins it around so now you don't know where the bullet is, and says, "I'm going to put this to your head and pull the trigger. Then in five seconds, I'll spin it and do it again. Then in five more seconds, again. If you aren't dead in thirty seconds, you can leave." Now you have to potentially die over and over for the next thirty seconds. That was the scenario I was presently experiencing. For the first time in my life, I thought I might die any second. The sound of my own heart was like a bass drum beating in my ears. I could feel the sweat rolling down my back, soaking the three layers of clothes I was wearing. Destruction was literally raining down from above and things were so far beyond my ability to save my own life I felt like I might be experiencing my last few breaths. Explosions burst over my head every few seconds, big ones. Explosions that were blowing things up the size of a city buses. I was in a tiny room in a small building, seemingly made out of paper-thin walls and an even flimsier roof. The explosions were so incredible they seemed to be taking place just a few feet above my crappy, little, makeshift fire department building. The blasts were so strong, I remember waiting for the roof to collapse, and being amazed that it hadn't. Why the glass wasn't shattering from the windows, I had no idea. How did my life come to this? What a shitty way to die.

It's funny where you find yourself sometimes, especially in the Air Force. You end up doing things and going places that "normal" people could never even dream was possible. It can be an exciting life if you are the type of person who allows themselves to be available to whatever life has to offer. Only five months earlier I was sitting in Arkansas with only 120 days left of my four-year tour. I had actually started packing my shit and making plans for what I was going to do when I became a civilian again. But then Saddam Fucking Hussein had to invade little Kuwait. Dick.

When that ass hat invaded his tiny neighbor to the south, I was actually on my way to Florida for a vacation. I was with my fiancée, heading south on I-75, when we started seeing people on the overpasses holding signs and banners and American Flags, supporting our troops. Then we started seeing convoys of Army vehicles heading different directions. Now, this was PRE-internet and cell phones so there was no real way to figure out what was going on other than turning on the car radio to find a station that was giving information. After surfing the dial, we finally learned Iraq had invaded Kuwait and America was ramping up. Honestly, I had no clue as to where Iraq or Kuwait were. I didn't know why this was important to the United States. But I was sure of one thing: if there was some crazy-ass war somewhere, firefighters sure as hell wouldn't need to go. Why would anyone send firemen (I was an Air Force firefighter) to a war/invasion or whatever the hell this was? Wars were all about *starting* fires and blowing the crap out of stuff, not putting out fires, right? Yep, I was that clueless.

But with the shit apparently hitting some fan somewhere, I decided to play it safe and pull over at the next exit to call my base and make sure my ass was still clear to head to Florida and enjoy surf and sand. I found a gas station with a pay phone and called my fire station. The Assistant Fire Chief, a man with seemingly zero sense of humor and personality, answered. "This is Sgt. White. I'm on leave (military speak for vacation) heading to Florida, and just wanted to check in because I saw a lot of Army vehicles on the road and the radio mentioned some invasion." Sgt. Pennington's monotone response was, "We have no information at this time if and when this will affect us. How can we reach you if we need to?" I gave him my hotel name and number, which was the best I could do. I was confident there was no way in hell a fireman was needed in some conflict in "bum fucked Egypt", and plus, I only had four months until I was out of the military. Who the hell would send someone into some "thing" when they only had four months left? No one is that stupid. You'd think after nearly four years of being in the military, I would have known better.

I'd just bore you if I told you about my vacation. It's Florida. I love Florida. Sun, beach, more sun. It was the middle of August and I was trying to use up the last of my vacation time before I was released from my four-year contract with the Air Force. I had plans to start college in January. Only two semesters to go for a Bachelor's Degree so I was pretty set in what I would be doing for all of 1991: finish my law enforcement degree and find a police job somewhere. As for my fiancée, Martha, I would play it by ear. Our relationship was up and down, and this little vacation was supposed to bring us together since things hadn't been so great lately. But we had four months to work on things before I left the military, so that would be nice. Right? Yeah, right.

We returned back to Northern Kentucky and I called the base again from my house, where my mom and step-dad lived. "COME BACK IMMEDIATELY" was the order, so I packed my shit, said my goodbyes and drove six hours back to Eaker AFB (Air Force Base), Arkansas. Eaker AFB sets in the northeastern corner of Arkansas. The base is next to the little town of Blytheville, which is between nowhere and no... fucking... where. You have to drive hours in any direction to be anywhere worth being. I had been here for about a year and a half and was ready to get the hell out. I know some people called this place home, but some people called it the asshole of America.

Some people.

I rolled in around 11:00 pm and hauled my bag into my dorm room to find my roommate, Drew, exactly where I had left him a week earlier: on his bed, watching my television. Drew was the laziest person I had ever met. Getting him off the bed and out the door required great skill. Only if there were some hope of being near a girl did he contemplate venturing out. Drew was also a firefighter, so I asked him to fill me in on what the hell was going on. He said the fire department was having some meeting tomorrow morning and both shifts had to be there to hear the news. I unpacked my bag, drank a beer and went to bed, clueless as to how my life was about to completely change.

Chapter 2
YOU WILL DIE......
PROBABLY

In the first few months of my Air Force career, I was given a nifty patch to sew on my uniform that said "Prime Beef". The military has all kinds of cool names to describe groups of people. PRIME BEEF sounded like one of the coolest groups someone could be in!

If I went to a steakhouse, "prime beef" meant the best, right?

What it actually meant was I was on a team of people who could (or at least should) be able to travel anywhere around the globe at a second's notice. Each person on the "prime beef" team had a bag packed with very specific items. Each bag was then squirreled away in some closet so when the call came, we just had to grab said bag and leap onto a plane. Sounds very impressive, doesn't it?

The next morning I received a very early phone call. "REPORT" to the fire department with our Prime Beef Bags. At 0800. In ONE hour. Rut Row. I knew my bag was buried in the deep, dark black hole of my closet, but I also knew that over the last few years of dragging this giant green duffel bag around, instead of going out to buy a new shirt or pants or other shit, I would just pull it out of my magical Prime Beef bag. I'd just replace it later. Eventually. One day. Really, why the hell did I need this stupid bag? I was a fireman, for God's sake. Who the hell needs a fireman to fly off to anywhere in a rush? If there is a fire somewhere, there must be firemen there already....right? Clearly, I had not thought this through.

For the next forty-five minutes, it was asses and elbows as I tried to grab old t-shirts and dirty uniforms to stuff into this PRIME BEEF bag. At one point, many moons ago, there was an actual list also stuffed in the "ready" bag describing all of the cool things that were supposed to be in there. I bet it had all kinds of interesting things listed like "flashlight" and "boots" and "six t-shirts" and "three

BDU pants." But what actually ended up in the bag was far different. The real test was to stuff as much crap into the bag as possible to make it look like it was filled with things once printed on some long-lost list, and then hope no one actually thought to inventory the bag at some point. It didn't really matter because I was leaving soon and this was obviously just a kind of drill to make sure we were "potentially" ready. We did have the cool patch on our uniforms after all.

One hour later we arrived at the fire department ('we' as in Drew and me; he wasn't on this team, he was there for moral support), told to drop our bags outside the Assistant Fire Chief's door and to report to him.

Cool. Just as long as no one actually looked in the bag. *That* was my biggest concern up to that point.

Ten of us smashed ourselves into his tiny-ass office and were somehow able to shut the door. Sergeant Pennington was a tall, thin, black man, and as far as I knew, never smiled. I hadn't spoken with him in any capacity for the last sixteen months, although I saw him nearly every day at work. In my non-medical opinion, he appeared to have some long, wooden device stuck permanently up his rear orifice. He sat there looking at the ten of us from behind his government-issued desk. He looked ticked off, more than usual, like someone just pissed in his beer. He told us we ten had been picked to leave on a Prime Beef Mission to support the invasion of Kuwait. He didn't know when we would leave, or if we would leave or where we would go if we even went.

His mastery of the details was overwhelming.

We needed to be available to leave at a moment's notice, and reminded us that if our bags needed anything extra, now was the time to get these items. Then he added this little tidbit, almost like he was hoping it would come true: "During past wars, more than half the men didn't come back, so look around and think about that."

WHAT THE FUCK WAS THAT?!?

Is that a real statistic?

Did he really need to say that??!!??

WAR?!? Who in their right mind sends FIREMEN to a fucking war?!?!?

And HOLD THE FUCKING PHONE, I'm out of the military in four months!

There had to be a mistake here.

With that, he told us to go home, but be ready to leave at any second and stay near a phone. As everyone filed out, I hung back because I wanted to make sure Sgt. Pennington realized THIS troop was supposed to be back in college in a very short time. "Yes, Sgt. White?", he said in his dry-as-desert-sand way of talking.

"Sgt. Pennington, I'm not sure if you were aware or not, but I'm due to separate (the term we use for leaving the military) in the first week of January. Maybe someone didn't realize that before they picked this team."

It was kind of a question, kind of a statement.

He just looked at me like I had made the most dumbass comment anyone has ever had the time to form and say out loud.

"Sgt. White, the orders are correct, go back to your dorm and await further orders."

Really? That's it? No discussion. Not even a little sympathy?

COME ON MAN, give me SOMETHING!

Nope.

I looked at him as he looked at me, so I turned around and left his tiny little island. I grabbed my sad, understocked duffel bag and headed back to my dorm. Dick.

I was apparently surrounded by them.

Chapter 3
This is all my fault

I loved my car. The first thing I did when I got back to the States from my last duty station in England was to buy this car. It was a 1990, Plymouth Laser, sixteen-valve, turbocharged, fuel injected, black, sleek, sexy, and *fast* rocket car. I washed it by hand at least once a week. I waxed it every few months. No piece of lint or dirt stayed inside the car for longer than it took for me to see it.

I *loved* my car.

If I was going to have to leave, I think I was going to miss my car more than anything else.

See where my head was?

As we pulled up to the dorms in Drew's red Mustang, I saw my car in its parking spot. I sighed. When I was in that car, behind that wheel, the world seemed to make sense. Right now, my world seemed like it was spinning down a dirty drain in a shared bathroom at the whorehouse. My plans were being sucked away at an alarming rate. I grabbed my bag and hauled it back into the room and immediately began rooting around in my closet and drawers to find crap to fill up my bag. Since I didn't have the slightest idea where I might be going, I put all kinds of stupid shirts, shorts, and pants inside. I tried to include as much of my military crap as I could find, but I figured if I didn't have it already, I'd get it later......somewhere......hopefully. When I had stuffed as much into my bag as it would hold, I decided I better call my mom in Kentucky and let her in on this predicament.

"Hi, Mom! I need to tell you some stuff."

"What's going on, Son?"

"Well, they say I might get deployed for whatever is going on and I might leave anytime in the next few hours to never, but I thought I better keep you up to date."

I was already starting to do some preliminary out-processing because I was due to leave the military soon, so I needed my mom's and stepdad's (also named Jim) help. "If I get deployed, I will probably need you guys to come get my car and as much of my stuff as you can take back home because whenever I get back, I'll probably be done with the Air Force and have to go home." My mom is (was) awesome, by the way. "What do you need us to do?"

I told her she would talk to my roommate, Drew, about when it would be a good time to meet up with him to get on base to pack up my stuff. It was a six hour drive from my house in Northern Kentucky to Eaker AFB, so I didn't want them to make this trip more than once. After I filled her in on the details, I told her I'd call her when and if I got the call to leave, but it would probably be a quick call.

"Bye, Mom, love you."

"Bye, Son."

The next call went to Martha, my lovely fiancée .

"Hi, I can't talk long, but I've been told I'm probably being deployed in the next few hours and when I get the call I have to leave immediately."

She was pissed.

"Why do YOU have to go?!?" she practically screamed at me.

"I'm on a deployment team, and I don't get a say. If I get the call to go, I'll have to leave immediately, so I'll try to give you a quick call to tell you whatever I can." Silence. More silence.

"Hello?" I knew she was there; I could hear her sisters talking in the background. She loved this "silent treatment" bullshit, and she knew I hated it.

"Martha, I have to get the rest of my stuff ready, I have to go. Bye."

Silence.

Fuck this!

"Look, I'll call you as soon as I know more, goodbye."

Silence.

"Goodbye Martha," and I hung up.

Oh man, I knew that pissed her off, but I didn't have time for her juvenile bullshit. I had stuff to do. Drew was watching me and listening in on my conversation with some amusement.

"I think she believes I volunteered for this deployment!" Drew just shook his head and laughed.

I told him my parents were going to come get my car and stuff and asked him to please help them when they arrived. Asking Drew to help perform some lifting or moving was like asking the sun not to shine, but I had to try.

He asked if he could drive my car while I was gone. WHAT?!? Was he serious?

"No, you have your own car!" He didn't like that answer, but he didn't pursue the matter. I felt like I had a million things to do, but didn't know where to start, so I just sat down and waited for the feces to accelerate into the blades of life. This was crazy.

Chapter 4
The Call

It was just about two hours from the time I left the fire department until the phone call came. It was Sgt. Humorless Pennington.

"Hello?"

"White, report immediately to the fire department with your GO bag...click".

"Yes ....", I started to answer before realizing he had already hung up.

Shit!

My heart started to race and my palms were instantly sweaty.

Double shit!

Now I had to call my mom and "her" again.

First Mom.

"Hi, Mom. They just called so I gotta go. I'm not sure when I can call again, but I will as soon as I can."

"Okay, Son, be careful," she said. I could tell she was a little scared.

"Bye, Mom, love ya."

"I love you, too," she said.

Now the shit call. I dreaded every number I punched on the phone, but I had to get this over with. Her mom answered. I quickly told her what was going on and asked to speak with Martha.

"Hello," she said dryly.

"I just got the call, I have to report immediately to the fire department. I'll call you to tell you more when I can."

Dead air.

"Martha, I gotta go now." I hung up. Geez us, crimany! What had I gotten myself into with this girl?

I grabbed my now fully-stuffed, green duffel bag and headed to the car. Drew drove again because I had a feeling that I wasn't coming back any time soon. Five minutes later I was back at the fire department, once again throwing my bag onto an ever-increasing pile of green bags. Sgt. "Good News" Pennington once again addressed us when the last of the ten of us finally arrived.

"You are scheduled to be deployed. The destination is Top Secret, so you are not being told where you are going until you are about to arrive. You will be getting on a bus in a few moments, taken to your aircraft, then deployed. We do not have information on how long you will be gone. SSgt Fox is the senior NCO (non commissioned officer) in your group and will be in charge. Do exactly as he says. Your friends and family are all waiting outside. From this moment on, you are not allowed to speak with them or make physical contact with them. Grab your gear, and proceed to the bus outside."

First, let me say that up until that point, I didn't really know SSGT Fox. He was on the opposite shift as me, so I rarely had reason to talk to him. From our brief encounters over the last year, he seemed like an ass, so I didn't make any effort to get to know him. As far as "friends and family" waiting outside, I didn't really have anyone. Drew was my roommate and buddy, so he was the closest friend I had for a few hundred miles. I felt bad for the married guys whose wives and kids were waiting.

This was regular, stupid military horse shit.

We didn't know a fucking thing to actually tell anyone, so why we weren't allowed to talk to them or shake hands or let the married guys kiss their family was idiotic. We didn't know exactly when we were leaving, where we were going, or how long we'd be gone! What TOP SECRET information did we have to pass on? We didn't even have any "interesting" information to pass on. We were more clueless than ever. Ugh.

Chapter 5
Death and Sex

We grabbed our bags and proceeded to the door. Once outside, we walked on the sidewalk next to the fire department and towards the concrete ramp that led to the airport flight line. The bus was about eighty feet away. Sure enough, friends and family were outside, kept back about fifty feet from us. Some were crying, some were waving, some were shouting "goodbyes," even some of the other firemen. The firemen weren't crying, just to be clear.

We were told we couldn't even yell back to them, not "I love you" or "Good-bye" or "Fuck you".

Just silent waves, it was fucking crazy.

One by one we threw our bags on the ground next to the shitty, old, green bus and filed in. Each of us took a seat as we looked out the windows to watch everyone looking at us like they may never see us again. Fucking spooky. This was really happening. I had this feeling in the pit of my stomach like "fuck man, maybe I'm NOT coming back!" Happy thoughts, happy thoughts, happy thoughts.

Once we were loaded up, we drove a short distance to a small building I really had never noticed. We were told to exit the bus and go into the building. I THOUGHT we were going to a fucking (we say fuck a lot in the military) airplane. Now what?!?

Once we all gathered inside, some officer handed us a paper and then gave us this juicy information: "Men, you are here to receive an ANTHRAX immunization shot. This is the first shot in a series of two. Your second shot will be administered later at your next station. This is an experimental shot. I cannot order you to take this shot. In order to be deployed, you must have this shot." WELL, SHIT! All we had to do was deny the shot and we could go home, right? Wrong.

He continued, "If you refuse the shot, you will be refusing your orders to be deployed and will spend the remainder of this conflict in military jail. You must sign the paper that was handed to you either accepting the shot or not accepting it."

He stopped talking. That was it.

He just looked at us and we all just looked at each other like we were waiting for the punchline to a really bad joke. Was he shitting us? Take a shot that could make me grow a third testicle, or maybe shrink up one I have already. OR.....go to jail. What kind of fucked up military logic was this?
Fuckity fuck fuck fuck.

I signed the fucking paper and stood in fucking line to take the fucking shot with every(fucking)one else. What the hell was ANTHRAX? Was I supposed to know this? We had watched a lot of crazy videos in Basic Training during our "gas mask" training, so maybe this was covered then....nearly FOUR YEARS AGO! Geez Us! What the hell was going on here?!? One by one we got the shot and looked at each other, wondering if we were all now part of some brotherhood of guys the military just fucked over, like the guys the military gave LSD to or made to watch nuclear explosions. Goddamnit!

We were immediately marched back on the bus, feeling a little numb, not from the shot, more from the shock of the circumstances. This was all just too crazy. We had no point of reference here so it was like some episode of *The Twilight Zone*. I had a feeling in the pit of my stomach that signaled dread. I'm usually the "gung-ho", adventure-seeking type. However, I knew the military was in charge of this little vacation, so my instincts were telling me the potential for stupidity was at DEFCON 2.

Our next bus ride was just as long as the last three-minute ride. We went straight to the flight line and parked just outside a KC-135. Our base had two kinds of airplanes. The first was the B-52 bomber, also known as the BUFF (Big Ugly Fat Fucker; hey, I didn't make it up!). Each BUFF of ours had several nuclear cruise missiles attached under each wing. Each B-52 could easily destroy the main cities of any country single-handedly and we had several planes equipped like this to blast off at a minute's notice. This is the kind of reality you see on a daily basis in the military and each of us has to come to some kind of grip with it in our own way. Most of us used humor because the alternative is to fall into some hole of black depression. It always amazed me they would make police officers take psychological exams and they would rarely ever use their gun during a career. However, military people never take these exams, but see death and destruction on a regular basis. Hmmmmm.

What I didn't know then, but realize now, is that if that test were actually given, we would have very few people in the military. Solely based on some of the people I met during my four plus years, some of these guys were nuts, but maybe "nuts" is the exact thing needed for the situation. But I digress.

The plane that was presently sitting in front of me was a KC-135, which was a "tanker", or "flying gas station". The middle of the aircraft, where passengers on a normal airplane would sit, was used to carry cargo but it was designed mostly to carry lots of extra jet fuel and to refuel other aircraft during flight. A person would lie down in the rear belly of the plane and look out a little window to watch other airplanes approach. The "boom operator" would then extend a long hollow "boom" to hook up to the other plane, and then "fill 'er up". I'm not sure why, but it never occurred to me that people ever used these planes to travel with, other than the crew. Today, I found out otherwise.

As we sat there looking at our plane, a vehicle drove up and an officer got out and entered our bus. Usually, when an officer enters a room or we encounter one, we stand and salute, but for some reason, sitting there on our military school bus, it didn't seem to enter anyone's mind to do exactly that. Which was funny, because a few seconds after he got on the bus, he said, "Just remain seated men." Maybe he was saving us from the faux pas, but I thought it was funny anyway. He introduced himself as Captain Somebody from the JAG (Judge Advocate General's corps). At first, that didn't ring a bell, because I had few encounters with these guys. This was the military's version of a law office so this guy was a military lawyer.

"Men," he said, "how many of you have your wills in order?"

My WILL?

For about three seconds I didn't even realize what he meant.

What? You mean as if when I DIE "will"?

Did Pennington put him up to this?

I slowly looked around at everyone else in the bus, and they had that same "what the fuck" look on their faces as well. We were a bunch of guys in our 20s and who the hell has a will in their 20s? No one spoke up.

"I'll take that as a 'no' then. Each of you take one of these documents and fill them out. I will sign and notarize them after you sign them. These basically state who you leave your assets and possessions to in the event of your death. If you are married, this is usually your spouse. If you are not married, you need to list someone, whether it is your parents or siblings. When you are finished, pass them to the front."

WAIT A FUCKING MINUTE HERE!

Whoa! Lawyer? Will? Death? What the hell was even going on here??? First, they make me take an experimental shot and threaten me with jail, then I'm signing my will? This was fucking crazy! This was beginning to feel like a ONE-WAY TRIP! Was I on Candid Camera? This was just some elaborate hoax to screw with Jim just before he was to leave the military. Right? Hahahahaha! Good one, guys!

But there were no cameras. By the looks on the faces of everyone else, they felt exactly how I did. Holy shit on a popsicle stick!

I looked at the paper, which had some legal-speak that would have taken an hour to read and understand. In the end, I just listed my mom as the person who would inherit all of my worldly possessions upon my demise. Upon reflection, I realized I didn't own jack shit: a car that was half paid for, a bird in a cage (named Bucko), some posters, and a second generation computer that was basically a glorified word processor. Fuck. I didn't have shit to show for my twenty-five years of being on planet Earth. How depressing. I signed the paper and passed it forward. The JAG officer collected them all, signed and stamped them, and said, "Good luck, men," then returned to his vehicle and drove away. Awesome. Could this day get any better? Wait.

Another vehicle pulled up and some guy, not an officer, got on board the Mr. Happy Bus and introduced himself. He was Sgt. Somebody Else (who can remember names) from some other place. I was a little numb at this point and not really paying attention. He had several small shoebox-sized boxes with him and began to pass them out to us. Now what? Maybe the urn to put our ashes in later, or maybe my Death Certificate? He said these were supplies to take with us, just in case we forgot to pack these essentials. I opened my box and peered inside. The first thing to catch my eye were two pairs of decent looking Ray-Ban sunglasses. Ok, that was cool. Toothbrush, toothpaste, and condoms?

Several condoms. Okay, where the hell were they REALLY sending us?!? If they knew I was going somewhere that required sunglasses and condoms, then this deployment was looking up mighty fast!

This guy was MUCH better than the last guy!

As I looked at the other guys, I could tell when they spied the condoms too, because of their shit-eating grins. There were some other odds and ends in the box, but the main events were already scored. I felt much better if for no other reason than my sense of humor was restored. I may die, and my mom may get all my shit, but apparently, I was gonna get laid too, so how bad could it get? Denial is wonderful.

Then things turned ugly.

The last guy to come on the bus was a hoot. This guy had a few large boxes with him. He introduced himself as Sgt Holy Shit and said he was from the NBC (Nuclear, Biological, Chemical) squadron, and was here to pass out our gas masks. Fuck. Gas masks?

It was gonna be hard to look cool in my new sunglasses while wearing a gas mask, let alone being able to use those condoms.

He gave each of us the same shitty-looking, used, sad-ass gas mask pouches that we had all trained with in Basic Training. These were the ones with two separate eye holes, a speaker in front and also two filters that could only be changed while it was off your face. This was the M-17 model, the same ones used during Vietnam, and whoever made it was a lunatic. These actually *looked* as if they had been used in Vietnam. If you needed to change your filters after extended use in a hostile, chemical filled environment, you had to hold your breath, close your eyes, quickly take this thing off, remove the old filters, replace the new filters in the interior pockets, put the mask back on and tighten it back up. Think you can do that knowing that if you take even one breath, your lungs will blister, or if you open your eyes you will go blind?

Here's where it gets either one degree above hilarious or one degree below insane. After all of us received our gas masks, Sgt Holy Shit informs us that the filters presently inside each mask are "training" filters and will not work in a gas-filled environment. He tells us as soon as we arrive at our final destination, be sure to see the NBC squadron there to get actual filters.

WAIT A FUCKING MINUTE! I had to ask the stupid question. "Uhhhhhh, what if we need to use these masks as soon as we arrive?" Everyone else was obviously thinking the same thing, but this guy just says, "Well, hopefully, that won't happen."

Then I asked the next obvious question, "Where are the chem suits that go with the masks?"

"They are on a pallet, loaded on the plane."

I didn't even ask how we are supposed to get to those. The obvious stupidity of this was overwhelming. This was just getting better by the minute. Fuck. Fuck. Fuck.

Chapter 6
Hi Ho, Hi Ho, It's off to Somewhere we go...

It was finally time to get this party started. Our bags had been thrown onto a pallet, strapped down and loaded into the plane. A rickety, portable staircase was pushed up to the aircraft so we could board. One by one we went up the stairs only to find that as passengers, we were secondary. The center of the airplane was made to haul cargo, and it was full from front-to-back and floor-to-ceiling with not only our pallet but small generators, crates and other crap I couldn't identify. Our "seats" were web seats that were folded against the side of the plane. We folded the bottom of the seat down and sat facing the center of the plane. There was so much stuff loaded, you couldn't see the guys on the other side unless you stood up and looked over the crates. If you had to put a "class" on the seating, it would be in the fifth-class range. Whatever. It just added to the adventure.

Eventually, all of the cargo was loaded, the doors were shut, we figured out how to use the seat belts, and the plane began to taxi. Normally while taking a flight on a commercial airplane, I'd look out the window and enjoy the view. This flight was obviously not "normal". Not only were we all facing the center of the plane, which is weird enough as the plane accelerates, but there were no windows, except for a tiny-ass one in the emergency door over the wing. So there we were, ten brave firefighters, stuffed onto a refueling plane sideways, with tons of cargo inches from our knees. I took a moment to look around, trying to gauge how everyone else was feeling. I noticed everyone's eyes were wide with concern. I wondered if I looked the same way. We were so far out of our element that it was darkly hilarious.

First Flight to the Unknown

Eventually, the bumps of the runway receded and at 1330 hours on August 27th, 1990 we were wheels-up into the great blue yonder. There was little-to-no talking between us. First, we were a bunch of guys, so we weren't big on conversation to begin with. Second, the engines were loud. We had been given little earplugs to wear since this plane was not insulated for passengers the same way commercial aircraft were. We mostly just looked at each other with that "deer in the headlight" stare. The muffled sound of the landing gear retracting into the plane put an exclamation point on the departure.

We were gone.

Arkansas was receding behind us, and we had no idea what was in front of us. We didn't even know what direction we were heading. It was like we were allowing ourselves to be kidnapped. In the back of my mind, I was excited though. I was going to take this as a welcomed break from a dismal relationship. I joined the Air

Force for adventure, and this was practically the living definition of the word. Time to start having fun.

I looked around the plane and finally took stock of the other guys with me. The only person who I knew much about was Robert Jones (Jonesy). Most people in the military have some kind of nickname, or at the very least were just called by their last name. Jonesy had bottle-bleached blond hair, a dark mustache, and believed he was God's gift to women, despite most women's overwhelming opinion to the contrary, but this didn't deflate him in the least. Jonesy had just married his girlfriend, who had recently graduated from high school in the nearby town, so technically, THE JONES was off the market. *Technically.* He was trying to pull off being "second in charge" of this group, but no one was taking him seriously, which just pissed him off more, and made it all the more funny to me. Jonesy, Drew, and I hung out when we were off-duty. I'm not even sure why except we were all outsiders to some degree; it was easier to just fall in together than try to make other friends.

Fox, our leader, was a married guy and appeared to like being in charge, but was not very good at it. Medium build, or maybe a few pounds heavy, he had the Hitler mustache and was quick to get flustered. He rarely smiled, and seemed pissed off constantly. Perfect guy to be in charge. I doubted we'd become close friends.

Van (Vanderson) was a tall guy with an eastern Kentucky accent, and by all indications was as dumb as a rock, but apparently, some women believed he was attractive. He, too, was married, but still enjoyed being ogled.

Mike Duncan (Dunc) seemed like a smart-mouthed, fun-loving guy, but he was married too, so he lived off base and I never really hung out with him. I came to know him as a master deal maker. If you needed some crazy, screwball mission accomplished, Dunc was your man.

Then there was Cowboy. Cow was on the opposite shift from me, so I didn't see him much past shift change each morning but that was enough to get a taste of what was coming down the pike. His southern charm and humor were mixed together in such a way that you never knew when he was being serious or putting one over on you. Every morning during shift change, one of us was tasked with giving some stupid "safety" speech. It could be about black ice, or heat exhaustion or whatever. Whenever it was Cowboy's turn, everyone paid attention. It was sure to be a doozy, and usually left the fire chief in such a state, you weren't sure if he was going to go ballistic with anger or explode from holding in the laughter. Given with a straight face and a twinkle in his eye, he would somehow make the dullest of topics a comic adventure. He gave one speech completely straight-faced about how to use condoms that had the entire fire department in tears. Thank goodness Cowboy was coming along.

Dunc and Cowboy were a team, like Martin and Lewis. They seemed to feed off each other, and once one got started, the other just joined in. It was so hilarious and perfectly timed, it seemed as if they had a comedy routine that had been practiced and refined. It was like watching a car chase on television. You didn't know where it would end up, but watching the twists, turns and jumps was great entertainment.

The rest of the guys were just faces and names since most worked on the opposite shift, and we just never hung out. Howard, Jeffries, Salyer, Day, and Idrizi. Maybe I'd get to know these guys. Maybe not. According to Pennington, half of us would die anyway, so what was the point?

Chapter 7
Super Quick History Lesson

If you don't know the details of Desert Shield/Storm (The Gulf War), there are plenty of books and documentaries to catch you up. This isn't a history book, this is one person's experience and how I dealt with it. The gist of the tale is this: Saddam Hussein, the leader of Iraq, felt like his country was getting screwed by Kuwait and other nearby countries. On August 2nd, 1990 his forces invaded the small, southern border country of Kuwait, quickly overrunning it within hours. The Kuwaiti leader, Jaber Al-Sabah, and most of his military made a quick retreat to Kuwait's southern neighbor, Saudi Arabia. On August 7th, the United States began sending troops and equipment into Saudi Arabia and by August 8th, the name "Desert Shield" had been given to this operation. For the next twelve days, all kinds of shit hit the fan. Sanctions and naval blockades are placed against Iraq; British nationals are taken hostage in Kuwait, and on it goes. The United States continues to send troops and equipment to Saudi Arabia, which brings you to August 27th, the day I stepped on to a plane bound for parts unknown. Isn't history cool?

Chapter 8
Pit Stops

About three hours after takeoff, we landed. One of the flight crew came back and announced that we were at Offutt AFB. Uhhhhh, where was that? Nebraska.

Nebraska?

Why were we in Nebraska?

Top Secret. Need to Know. Hush Hush. Don't ask stupid questions.

Which questions were stupid?

All questions are stupid because you are asking them, and you aren't supposed to be asking questions, you idiot.

We will tell you shit when we decide you need to know it.

Everyone kept asking Sgt. Fox if he knew what was going on, but he kept telling us he was completely in the dark, however, the look on his face indicated he knew more than he was telling. I was convinced he was just being an ass and knew zero but wanted us to think he knew more. After the plane finally came to a stop, some poor, clueless airman came onto the plane and told us he would be taking us somewhere we could wait and get something to eat. We immediately started bombarding this poor guy with a hundred questions.

Where exactly where were we going?

How long would we be here?

Where was our stuff?

He finally stopped us and explained that he knew absolutely nothing other than he was to pick us up and take us to a building. He was told to keep us away from other people. Oh, for God's sake! We were just a bunch of firemen from Arkansas, why were they treating us like we had the nuclear launch codes?

It was about 330pm local time when we were loaded on to a little bus and taken to a building on the base. We were hustled off and taken into what looked like a small conference room with no windows. We kept asking the airman questions, but he assured us that he knew absolutely nothing, except to tell us that we must stay in the room. He would bring us food and beverages as soon as possible.

Only pic I took in our little room in Nebraska. I think I was the only one with a camera. No image preview back then.

Fox also continued to be a dick. We'd ask him, "Do you know where we're going?," and he would answer with, "I can't tell you where we are going."

Did that mean he didn't know or he did know but wasn't allowed to tell us?

His face began to turn darker shades of red the more we badgered him until he started yelling at us to stop asking him questions. Most of us had little-to-no regard or respect for what slight rank he had above us, so the authority he was trying to assert was useless.

Some of us had to use the bathroom so as soon as our clueless airman returned we let him know the situation. He told us where the bathroom was but told us we could only go two at a time. This sounded like grade school rules. Geez! Just getting out of this stupid room was going to be a treat. When it was my turn, Jonesy and I walked down the deserted hallway to the bathroom, but I noticed just outside our door was a pay phone on the wall. Once we got back to the room, I informed the other guys about the phone. Could we make a call? Most of us decided we were calling home, and poor Fox's head looked like it was about to explode while trying to decide if it was okay or not. I knew his real dilemma; he wanted to call home himself, but if he did that, he couldn't justify not letting the rest of us. Finally, the little airman couldn't find anyone to say "yes or no" and Fox finally gave in after we convinced him that because we knew absolutely nothing anyway, making a call home was completely harmless. We each had five minutes to make a call. While waiting my turn, the airman returned with boxed lunches. The chow hall made us sandwiches, with a bag of chips and a soft drink, so I chewed my way through the bounty. Eventually, it was my turn to make a call.

Mom or Martha?

Both. I called mom first. She would be worried, not pissed off, so that felt like a good way to start.

"Hi, Mom, I'm in Nebraska."

"Why are you in Nebraska?" she asked.

"We're getting a different plane I think and going somewhere else, but we don't know where. I'll call you as soon as they tell me something that I'm allowed to tell you, and if there is a phone."

"Okay, call me as often as you want."

Moms are great. We said our goodbyes and then I made the call I didn't really want to make. I really just hoped she wasn't home and I could talk to her mom or one of her many sisters.

Why was I even calling? I guess I'm a glutton for punishment.

I used my AT&T calling card and dialed her number. Her mom answered. I could tell she was actually concerned about me and started asking me questions. I told her they were keeping us in the dark about where we were going and I really didn't have any information. I told her I only had a minute or two to talk, so she put Martha on the phone. "Look, I'm sharing this one pay phone with nine other guys, so I don't have much time to talk."

Dead air.

"I'm in Nebraska and we are going somewhere else after this, but they aren't telling us yet. Are you there?"

"Yes, I don't understand why you have to go! You're getting out in four months!"

"Martha, this is the military. I don't get to make those decisions."

She sniffed. Was she actually upset? Who could tell.

"Look, I'll call you again when I'm able, I gotta go. I love you (Did I?), bye."

She actually said, "bye" back. Her mom probably gave her hell about the last conversation we had. I hung up and went back to the room.

With the new sense of freedom using the phone had given us, we felt it was time to push the limits a little more. We asked our liaison airman if we could go to the BX (think military Walmart). All of us left Arkansas with less than adequate supplies, so this could be our last chance to stock up. After about forty-five minutes, he came back with a surprising "yes". We could go to the BX. He would walk us over, and we were limited to thirty minutes, then it was back to "the room".

Really, the sequestered thing was just getting stupid. We were on a military base, and knew less than zero, so who exactly were we going to tell anything?

The BX was fairly small, more like the size of a WalGREENS than a WalMART, but it was better than nothing. I thought it was a good time to get a few more t-shirts. But then one of the guys heard from someone in the BX that everyone was being sent to some desert, and there were *sand fleas*, so if you didn't want to be eaten alive by *fleas*, you better get some OFF!

Oh shit!

All of us started running around looking for the OFF, but there was none left, so these Einsteins starting buying dog and cat flea collars. What the hell did they plan on doing with these things? I could just picture these idiots walking around with flea collars on. I refused to buy them, so I left with just a few stupid little items to get me to the next place we ended up, hopefully somewhere with a beach and some cold beer. Sunglasses and condoms, right?!? Hahahahahaha.

Chapter 9
Onward and Upward

Our delightful young airman came back into our room with news. Our cargo was being loaded on to a C-141 aircraft, and sometime in the not-too-distant future, we would be boarding as well. Our cargo was comprised of two pallets. On the first were our duffel bags and chemical warfare suits (we hoped) and all our uniforms, boots, underwear, and anything else we were going to need for a short-to-extended stay anywhere. The second pallet contained crates that held brand new M-16 rifles. These were so new, they even had the plastic caps on the ends of the barrels. They had never been shot. They had never been sighted in.

We were firemen, in case you've missed that fact up to this point.

Firemen with M-16s.

I know, I know, we had all qualified, at some distant point in time, during Basic Training, with this rifle. As I pondered this fact and then pictured the group of guys I was presently with, I could only hope we never had to actually use these firearms. I'm not sure some of these guys could be trusted with a slingshot, let alone a military-grade rifle. Sometime before we left, we were told to make sure we sighted in the rifles once we arrived at our final destination.

We seemed to be going somewhere about half-prepared. Gas masks that didn't work, hazmat suits we couldn't access, rifles that had never been tested or sighted. Truthfully, I don't think they even sent bullets with us anyhow, so the rifles were moot. We impatiently waited for someone to tell us it was time to leave.

Finally, at 9pm, we were told it was time to go. We all had that "I'm worn out from traveling" thing going on, but we grabbed our little bags and left for the short ride out to our new-to-us plane. We stopped in front of a C-141. I'd previously flown on just a handful of Air Force aircraft. You'd think that being in the Air Force, we'd be flying everywhere, all the time, on jet fighters and cargo aircraft and everything in between. The sad truth was that unless you are on a flight crew, you really didn't have many opportunities to fly in an honest-to-goodness Air Force plane. My training had put me on several aircraft before. Firemen had to know how to make entry into airplanes, shut them down in case the crew was incapacitated, use the onboard fire suppression systems, remove safety constraints from the crew and passengers, and then remove those people from the aircraft. A few years earlier, while stationed in England, I was sent for a two-week class to learn Aircraft Rescue Firefighting. It was during that class that I was able to board and practice on a large variety of planes. It was a challenging class, but loads of fun. I received my Rescue Certificate when it was finished. That was a long time ago. Now I was finally going to ride in one of these babies!

The "C" in C-141 stands for "cargo", which means the primary mission of this aircraft is to move cargo. It's like the eighteen-wheeler of the Air Force. The rear of the plane opens wide to allow large pallets or trucks to be loaded and flown all over the planet. Just as with the last plane, the seats today were against the side of the cargo area, and the middle was loaded with as much as they could cram inside. This plane sits low, so no need for rickety stairs this time. We stepped inside and saw the crew had left just enough room near the front of the cargo area for us to push the web seats down. The rest of the plane had generators, trucks, and piles of more unidentified crap on pallets that I didn't care about. I just hoped whoever loaded this thing made sure to load *our* crap on there somewhere. We took our seats, and the crew chief handed us all a brand new set of earplugs. It's hard to complain about commercial flying after doing it this way a few times. He then gave us some instructions as to where the sad little toilet was, and that we'd be given something to eat after takeoff. One of us asked if he knew where we were going, but he smiled and said he was told that was information he could not pass along. Fox gave us all the stink eye for even asking. Screw you, dude.

Soon, the door was closed, the engines fired up to a high pitch, and we taxied down to the end of the runway. When we finally started down the runway, we were in the same predicament as before. We had no windows, and even if we did, it was almost 10pm and there was nothing we could see if we could look out, except for the last glimpses of the United States that we'd know for several months. I wanted to feel excited, but I just felt exhausted, and from what I could see, everyone else felt the same way. It had been a long fucking day.

Chapter 10
No Bull

If you think it's hard to get comfortable in an economy seat on Delta, you haven't lived until you've flown for nine hours in a web seat. You can't lay down, and slouching just gets you a metal bar in the ass. After about thirty minutes in the air, the crew chief passed out our dinners, but it was the same damn box lunch we had a few hours ago. Some white bread sandwich, chips, and a juice box. I'm pretty sure there was a fudge brownie too. It was either eat it or throw it away, and I was so hungry I just devoured every crumb. Soon we all started getting cold and noticed the metal floor was getting a thin layer of ice on it. The crew chief came back out and told us that the higher we could get in the plane, the warmer we would be. Since we had left Arkansas in late August, we were all dressed for the heat. Now we were all putting on every stitch of clothing we had. Almost everyone started climbing onto the pallets to find some comfortable position that was higher than the web seats. Not your average flight, and the "leave your seatbelt on during flight" was nonexistent. It was more "every man for himself."

About three or four hours into the flight, the crew chief came back and asked if anyone was interested in going to the cockpit to see something really cool?

Hell, yeah!

To get to the cockpit from the cargo area, you had to climb a small ladder and then go through the door, which was a few feet above the cargo bay. We went up and back two at a time. When it was my turn, I was like a kid in a candy shop. I love planes, and getting to go up to this cockpit deck during the flight was awesome. The crew was watching us closely as we entered, looking to see the expression on our faces as we caught a view of the windshield.

There was this magical blue ball of electricity, about the size of a softball, sitting on the outside of the windshield. Then, coming out of the ball were blue spider webs of electricity.

All I could say was, "Cooooooool," since these guys didn't seem concerned. "So, what is it?" I asked.

The pilot told us it was called St. Elmo's Fire and was caused by a buildup of static electricity on the body of the airplane. He said it was harmless to the aircraft. We stood there and watched the little webs of electricity arch around like some crazy science experiment gone wild. We didn't even bother to ask the crew about our destination since it had become clear nobody was allowed to tell us anything yet.

After dozing on and off for the next several hours, I checked my watch. It was about 6am, or at least that's what time it was in Arkansas. That meant we had been flying for about eight hours, but I had no idea in which direction. Were we gaining or losing time zones? The sun was up, but in my foggy state, that didn't mean anything to me. A few minutes later, the crew chief came back in and asked for our attention. Everyone who was sleeping began waking up from the nooks they had squeezed themselves into or on top of.

Once he was sure we were listening, he shouted (remember the ear plugs and loud engines?), we were beginning our descent into Terrejon AFB and would be on the ground in less than an hour.

Someone yelled, "Where is Terrejon AFB?"

"Spain," he yelled back.

Spain?

"Is that our last stop?", someone else yelled.

Fox was looking snarky, like he knew the answer but was getting pissed off we were asking questions. The Chief answered, "You'll be given information when we land." That sucked as an answer.

The plane landed and taxied to one end of the taxiway. The chief told us it was 1405 hrs local, which made the flight just over nine hours. Man, that sucked. Lots of things sucked apparently. We all looked like shit and smelled equally bad. The door to the airplane opened and the harsh light and heat hit us instantly. Since the inside of the plane felt like a meat locker, it made the heat from the outside feel like we opened an oven door. A few minutes later an Air Force guy came on board and gave us our next bit of information.

This was like some kind of stupid global adventure game where they only gave you one clue every flight. The sad part was this was only a layover. There was a hangar nearby that we would walk to after deboarding. Inside the hangar were cots. Find a cot, relax until we are told what to do next. *Do not attempt to leave the base!* Great. I'm in Spain and can't go sightseeing?

Truthfully, I was beat from the shitty traveling conditions and the time changes so leaving the base didn't sound that exciting anyhow. The ten of us gathered what little crap we had and started walking the 300 yards towards the expansive hangar. Everything I saw was sand-colored. The buildings, the hangar, the vehicles. Everything. It didn't feel like Spain. For a moment, I actually doubted we were in Spain at all. It was just a lie so we really didn't know where we were. *Top secret*! Just peachy.

This hangar could easily have fit a 747 inside. Both doors stood wide open, and on the left side were hundreds of cots set up in very neat rows and columns. Few of them were occupied, so I supposed we were some of the first to use these facilities. It seemed they were expecting a lot of people here at some point.

As we walked inside, we each found a cot to throw our stuff on. Our "guide" told us the Red Cross had set up some booths on the other side of the hangar with items we might need. Since almost all of our stuff was packed away on some pallet, we all made a beeline straight towards the booth. We were greeted by several smiling women wearing the standard Red Cross uniforms. They had pre-made bags of items they began handing each of us. I peeked inside to find soap, razors, and a little hand towel. I just had to smile. It's funny what little treasures presented at the right time can do for your morale. It felt like Christmas!

They pointed us towards the bathrooms as if they knew what our next question would be. Once inside, everyone stripped off their uniform shirts and began taking "sink baths." We washed up and shaved as well as a person can in a sink. Man, that felt good! We had to put back on the same shitty t-shirts, but we only smelled half as bad now, and my attitude improved a great deal. We made our way back to the cots to chill out and hopefully find out what was to be done with us and to us next.

Fox was unaccounted for, so we supposed he must be somewhere finding out our next flight info. I laid on the cot and looked at the top of the hangar, which seemed to be a hundred feet high. This was the first actual rest in what seemed like a lifetime. I realized the doors to the hangar were wide open in hopes of catching any breeze that might happen by. It would have needed to be a hell of a breeze, more like a tornado, to cool this place down. The air was hot, and I felt the beads of sweat forming on my forehead. I must have been more tired than hot though because I drifted off for about an hour until I could hear some of the guys bombarding Fox with questions. It seemed some of the more vocal guys like Cowboy and Dunc thought Fox was full of shit and knew more than he was telling.

"Look Fox, just tell us where we're going!" The "you motherfucker" was implied, I felt. At least that was the tone I took it as. Cowboy was trying to persuade Fox into telling what he knew.

"It's not like we can tell anybody shit, so just tell us what you know," but Fox's face just kept getting redder and redder, and the heat wasn't helping.

"All I can tell you is that we are waiting for our plane to be fueled and loaded," and he walked away. There were plenty of grumbles and names called under people's breath. It was obvious no one even remotely respected Fox. If this were a ship, I'd have said a mutiny was close at hand. This cloak and dagger bullshit was getting old. We were worn out, hot and getting pissed off, not a good combination in the best of circumstances. Jonesy actually tried to smooth it over with everyone, telling us that, "Fox will tell us stuff when he knows it or is allowed." Jonesy was trying his best to be "second in command", but it was a joke, and no one paid him even the slightest bit of notice. Poor Jonesy. He desperately wanted to be the "cool" guy with power, but he just wasn't up to the task. We all just plopped down and waited.

Around 6pm, Fox came walking towards us like he was on a mission; he must have information he could actually share with us.

"Ok," he started, "We have a plane and we will be taking off in about an hour. Don't go anywhere and be ready to move when they come for us."

Naturally, the first question was, "Where are we going?"

There was that fucked-up look on his face again.

Did he not know? Did he know and couldn't tell us? Did he know and refused to tell us because he's a little dictator? All he would say was, "That's all I can tell you," and he left again to whereabouts unknown. I think he didn't hang around with us because he didn't want to endure any further angry questions. I was happy that I was just one of the guys and not in charge of anything because being in charge looked like it sucked.

Chapter 11
Flying starts with "F"

Jonesy and Fox just before takeoff. Notice yummy box lunch next to Jonesy.

Just after 7pm we were "wheels up", putting Spain in the rear view mirror. I'd been to Spain during a vacation I took back in 1988. I wasn't impressed with it then and this time it left an even less friendly and exciting taste in my mouth. I wasn't disappointed to be heading out. The big question was *where will we land next*, followed quickly by *will we stay there or keep this hopping around lifestyle*? We were again on a C-141, crammed inside with loads of equipment. Was it the same one? I didn't think so. If it was, they offloaded and reloaded some equipment. I didn't really care. No sense of direction, no information and a dwindling sense of humor. The sun eventually went down, and we were left with the dim lights inside the cold interior once again. Ears plugged, all we could hear was the engines outside. We didn't talk because (1) we're guys, remember, and (2) what was there to talk about? Fox wasn't giving up any information and we were done guessing or harassing him. All we could do is wait. Wait until we landed in some new country and deal with whatever was thrown at us next. I drifted off, slumped in my web seat, my back deciding to complain later when I woke up.

About five hours later, I woke up as the crew chief yelled we would be landing soon. My toes were cold, and I think there was ice on my boots. The guys had again found different areas to try to sleep, so everyone began to make their way back to their seats. As we began to feel the plane descend, the chief told us to pay attention. He looked concerned. That wasn't good.

"We are about to land in Riyadh, Saudi Arabia." (Local Time 322am)

Oh, *that* sounded exciting.

"We will be performing a *combat landing*, which means we will be coming in steep and landing fast. There are several terrorist cells in this city. As soon as we land, and the door opens, you will run to the area we direct you to."

HOLY SHIT! What the fuck was THAT all about?!?

I looked around and everyone's eyes were now wide-fucking open. Man, I hoped we didn't have to use these fucked up chemical warfare masks. This was turning out to be a good 'ole fashioned, military cluster fuck.

Combat landing?

Terrorists?

Run for your life?

Geezzzz us!

This was NOT in the brochure for being a firefighter!

He did not sell this landing short on what would really happen. I wondered if these pilots were getting a kick out of scaring the shit out of the ten, poor firemen. Sure enough, we descended like we were about to crash, then pulled level at the last second and taxied like a drag race to a fast stop. The brakes on this bird must have been about to burst into flames. Suddenly the door flew open and the crew chief starting yelling, "Go! Go! GO!," like we were parachuting over Normandy.

There was darkness outside, but the crazy oven heat hit me like a bitch slap from next Tuesday.

It was THIS fucking hot at 3am? Holy shit balls!

There was some other guy outside on the ground yelling for us to follow him as he went sprinting away. Fuck! We all took off out of the plane one after the other, trying to catch this unknown dude. Running fast after sitting for hours inside a cold plane wasn't working out very well. Weren't we supposed to zig and zag back and forth like John Belushi so the terrorists couldn't take us out easily? We ran after this guy for about a hundred yards until we came to the edge of the tarmac and went through a gated fence door. We all stopped after the gate slammed behind us. I didn't hear any shots while we were running, so maybe the terrorists were so impressed with our great speed that they decided not to waste the bullets.

Fat chance. If anything, they couldn't hold the gun still because of all the laughing they were doing at our pathetic sprint. Hey, whatever keeps you alive.

Most of the guys were bent over with their hands on their knees, trying to catch their breath. That was probably the farthest and fastest most of them had run in years. The guy who had lead us out of the "kill zone" waited for the heavy breathing to stop before letting us know where we were exactly, and what would happen next.

Sgt. Somebody began, "This is ELF1," he said as he gestured all around us with his hand. ELF1? What kinda screwy name was that? Was it near SANTA3 and PRANCER14? The military sure loved to name shit in ways you'd never dream up. I took a look around, but because it was dark and there were very few lights, all I could see was some crappy shack-like buildings and some tents. Was this *all* of ELF1, or was I just seeing the only forty feet of an entire complex my eyes could make out?

"Who is in charge?" he asked.

Fox rose his hand, declaring himself Emperor, and spoke up, "I'm Sgt. Fox," he said.

"Fox, come with me, the rest of you can relax."

Shit. That was it? Run like hell, and then Fox goes off to get information? Ugh. Why was I even surprised? It was the military. They loved this crap. Some of the guys started to ask questions, but Sgt. Somebody just said, "We will brief Sgt. Fox and he will brief you when he returns."

Lovely.

Chapter 12
Knowledge is Power

Outside, standing around, sitting on pallets (there was never a shortage of pallets), or lying on the ground, we waited. Fox was gone for well over an hour; so long that it was beginning to get light from dawn. In my mind, there was no fucking way that Fox was getting briefed *that* much information for him to be gone so long. I just pictured him inside, sitting on some nice couch, air conditioning blowing like a hurricane, relaxing with veiled belly dancers, as we poor, overheated idiots sat outside waiting for his dumb-ass to grace us with his presence and information. I barely knew this guy, but he had already become a dick in my mind. As it eventually turned out, I was proven right on several occasions, but at this point, I was just going with my gut.

He finally came back out, drunk and smelling like a whore house (maybe I'm exaggerating here) and as we began to bombard him with questions, he held up his hands as if to block the words flying at him. His face turned red again to signal he was mad, or embarrassed, or an ass, and said, "I just got briefed by the commander," which got our attention, so we quieted down. Fox continued, "We need to stay here until the Star Flight comes back later today. It's a C-130 that makes flights between here and Oman. We need to stay here so we don't miss the flight."

Okay, where was this Oman? I barely knew where Saudi Arabia was on a map, and none of us had a clue where or what an Oman was.

Someone asked what we were all thinking, "Where's Oman?"

Fox looked annoyed at the question, but until someone pulled out a map, I bet his dumb-ass didn't know where it was either.

"It's south of Saudi Arabia, on the coast," he said.

Did he say *coast* as in *beach*? Because I could get on board with hanging out on a beach for however long this thing was we were doing.

As the sun peeked over the horizon, we were finally able to see exactly what our surroundings were. We were obviously at an airport. King Fahd Airport to be exact. We seemed to be in a small, makeshift, hastily constructed encampment of shack-like buildings and tents. The shacks were probably already here, but the tents were apparently put here by us. ELF1 was its name, which I remembered from being told hours earlier, but it really didn't mean much at the time. We had no idea what was beyond ELF1. All we could see were the airport runways and the tents and shacks directly surrounding us. Our world was very small right now. All I knew was this area looked like a hellhole, and as soon as we could get our asses on that C-130 and to a place where those sunglasses and condoms could come in handy, the better.

Beach, here I come!

We just had to hunker down here for a few hours.

Fox kept disappearing for an hour here and an hour there, claiming to be checking on updates. I knew it was bullshit, and that he was having a breakfast of pancakes and sausages, fed to him by women in veils. Bastard. We all felt like the forgotten stepchildren. No one was paying us any attention, and stupid Fox was our only lifeline to information. Eventually, Fox returned just before noon with some bad news. As he wiped the bacon grease from his mini mustache with one of the colorful veils, he informed us the Star Flight for today was cancelled. We were being given our duffel bags and sent to a hotel in downtown Riyadh until the next Star Flight returned in a few days. Until then, we had to lay low and wait.

Uh oh, that didn't sound good.

We didn't have a choice in the matter though, so we collected our bags and followed Fox and another Sgt to some waiting vehicles.

Chapter 13
Strangers in a Strange Land

It was around noon, and we could all tell that we weren't in Kansas anymore, or even Arkansas for that matter. The heat here was all-consuming, like living inside of an oven. You could feel the radiation of the sun on exposed skin. Why the hell did anyone live in a place that felt like this? We drove through the airport/base, and into the city. The construction of buildings all looked weird. I'd been to plenty of different countries over the last three years, but this one was like Mos Eisley on Tatooine from Star Wars. Brown, sand-colored buildings mostly. Weird architecture. Everything just seemed *not right*, but being the adventurous type, I just chalked it up to a different culture and their way of life. Other than the strange ways they dressed, I couldn't make out much more. We stopped in front of the White Palace Hotel and unpacked our bags to the sidewalk. The Sgt took us inside and procured three rooms for us. The last thing he said to us before leaving us to our own devices was, "Don't drink the water," and he was gone.

Don't drink the water? Why?!?

He never explained more. Off we went in search of our rooms.

Good ole White Palace Hotel. Fresh off the plane.

Fox announced since he was in charge, he was making the command decision to take a room all to himself, leaving the nine of us to cram into the other two rooms. Just one more reason to confirm he was a first class dickhead. We found our rooms on the third floor and discovered each room only had one queen sized bed. Feeling rather fucked, we told Fox this was a load of shit, but he had his room and couldn't care less. He sauntered off saying, 'Do not leave this hotel." We were too tired to argue, for now. I suggested throwing the top mattress on the floor and making two beds, which is exactly what happened. Still not the best situation, but it beat the alternative.

A few of us immediately collapsed on the beds, while a couple opened the balcony door to stand outside and look at the city from this vantage point. Brown. Lots of shades of brown for as far as the eye could see. We knew absolutely nothing about Saudi Arabia, except for Lawrence of Arabia, a movie from 1962. From the few movies I could remember, the people wore long robes and funny headdresses, but that seemed like some stereotype from long ago, so I was sure that modern times had caught up with these people. Suddenly, and without any warning, speakers all over the city started blaring some guy singing in a terrible voice. It scared the crap out of all of us, and we looked at each other in dismay until someone said, "What the fuck is THAT?"

This weird sing-song chant kept going for a couple of minutes and stopped as quickly as it had begun. What had just happened?

We started smiling and laughing at the craziness of the situation. Crammed in tiny rooms, can't drink the water, can't leave the hotel, and not really knowing what was going to happen next. Everyone was exhausted, and it was a couple of hours until the hotel served dinner, so everyone collapsed to sleep for a few hours, hoping that the crazy singing didn't start again anytime soon.

I was excited about dinner, probably way more excited that I should have been. I was looking forward to hot food that didn't come out of a glorified shoe box. As we made our way to the dining room, I noticed a few men in the lobby, all wearing the "Arabian costumes". They had on the long white, one-piece pullover with buttons up the front. They also had

View from the hotel balcony. Pepsi in English and Arabic.

on the red and white checkered headdress with a little black ring around it to hold it on. Each wore it in a slightly different style. Some had one side flipped over, another let it just hang down around their face, while another man had both sides flipped back. I guess it was their version of how to wear a baseball hat.

We finally made it to the dining room, where we could discuss this interesting fashion show we had just encountered. Remember the "no water" rule? Well, we all ordered soft drinks but didn't even consider the ice was made from the water. The actual food ordering was more pointing at the menu and hoping we were asking for actual food. The English subtitles of the Arabic descriptions were not very helpful. There was no steak or much else that looked like something you would expect from any other restaurant in the world.

In the end, I'm pretty sure I had my first taste of goat. We would have to get better at this menu if we were going to survive here for very long.

It wasn't until we were walking back up to our rooms that the ice cube problem occurred to me.

Oh shit!

What was going to happen to us now? The locals apparently drank the

water, so how bad could it be? For the next two days, I don't think anyone pooped. Maybe it was the water or two days of traveling and eating boxed food, but from that point on, I tried to avoid the ice.

As soon as we walked into our rooms, the screaming/chanting started blaring through the city, and once again, it scared the bejesus out of all of us.

Fuck! How often did this bullshit happen?

Cowboy showing off one of our Five Star luxury rooms.

The next day was spent entirely in the hotel. Fox said he was calling the base every few hours to find out when the next Star Flight out of this shithole was due to show up. If they said we needed to leave immediately, we had to be ready to haul ass and go, so we were stuck.

We soon found out what the chanting lunatic on the big speakers around the city was doing. It was the call to prayer, and happened five times a day. We didn't figure out the schedule, but each time it happened, we jumped just a little less. Eventually, it would become like planes flying overhead. You knew it was happening, but it just became background noise. Eventually.

So we ate their weird food, walked around the lobby, found phones and called home, and looked out our balconies at the city. We didn't hear any gunfire or see terrorists running in the streets. In fact, it looked like a normal city, except for the weird architecture. Cars were driving back and forth, people were walking around, planes were flying overhead. We were stuck in a hotel.

By the third day, we'd had enough. Instead of asking Fox to leave, we told him we were venturing out of this fucking hotel. There was a pet shop directly across the street, and we told him that we were going over to take a look. It seemed pretty harmless. We hadn't seen anyone abducted in front of the hotel, and if the big call for the Star Flight came, we could certainly be back fast enough that it wouldn't make a difference. I think we just wore him down really and he just said, "okay."

Half of us, the adventurous ones, went across the street. As we crossed the street, I tried to take a look around and get a feel for my surroundings. Most of the men outside were wearing the same clothing as the dudes we saw in the hotel. We saw zero women. Hmmmm.

As we walked in the "pet shop" we immediately noticed things were a bit off. You could buy all sorts of crazy-ass animals in this place you wouldn't find in the USA. Monkeys, sheep, birds, and some animals I didn't recognize.

Dorothy, we *definitely* were not in Kansas anymore.

We were like little kids in this place. One of us would discover some weird creature and yell for everyone to come see it until someone else found an even stranger animal. It felt more like a zoo than a pet store, except the animals were all for sale. We were laughing our asses off and wondering how we could justify buying a monkey as we left the place to tell the guys across the street of our adventure. But the big news was just down the street.

As we crossed the road back to the hotel, I saw a Burger King about a hundred yards away. But I didn't really see Burger King, what I saw was a little island of the USA. I saw home.

Chapter 14
Whopper

We were tired of this goofy-ass food the hotel was serving. Mystery meat at its finest. Honestly, there wasn't one meal I'd had that we actually knew what meat we were eating.

But I had a plan now.

In fact, it was more of a group movement than a personal plan.

Once we informed everyone of Burger Heaven just a few feet from our very front door, a movement was afoot. At first, Fox was against this new idea. This wasn't just across the street, but now we wanted to go about a block away. He was under some impression that either we would be assaulted by terrorists or we would cause some international incident.

Personally, I believed the second possibility was much more likely. Dunc had some wild look in his eye like he just wanted to make something explode and Cowboy just seemed to what to do whatever it was that would piss Fox off the most. I thought the entire situation was amusing, so besides wanting to taste my American burger, I was all in on whatever caused Fox's face to turn multiple shades of red and purple.

Once again, Fox gave in, so I quickly discovered that under the right circumstances, we could manipulate our "leader." We could explore the King of Burgers in two groups. With money in hand that we had just exchanged at the hotel lobby, off we went in search of burgers and fries. The walk down the street felt good. It seemed the further away we got from that hotel, the better I felt. We eventually stood in front of *The Home of the Whopper*, or as I read it, *The Land of the Free, Home of the Brave,* but things were not as they should have been. There were two front doors, each with a special sign, written in both Arabic, and English. One said "Family Entrance", the other said, "Males Only".

I had no idea what was going on, but since we were all guys, we just went in the door on the right, "males only." There was a dividing wall after we opened the door, but it stopped at the order counter in front of us. At the counter, we could easily see the "family side" but I got the idea gawking was frowned upon. While waiting my turn to order, I nonchalantly tried to see the other side, just to understand why exactly we were forbidden to be over there. From the few people I could see, there seemed to be a few families sitting at tables eating. Some of the people, women I guessed, were wearing the full black garments from head to toe and were lifting some veil when they took bites of their food. The kids, both male and female, seemed to be wearing typical, American style kids' clothes, and the men/boys were wearing the male style of clothing we had seen all the other men wearing so far. When it came my turn to order, I just said, "Whopper, fries, and Coke." Apparently, this guy taking my order had heard these famous words a million times and rang me up. The cash register showed some mystery numbers, so instead of trying to figure out the money, I just handed the guy the largest bill I had and hoped he gave me back the right change. I'd figure out this money thing later, if needed.

Hopefully, we'd be on some beach any day now, and that country might have an entirely new money system, so why burn brain cells trying to figure this system out?

Soon, our to-go orders were handed to us, and back we went to The White Palace in our quest to prove we could walk down the street, order food, find our way back, and not die. We told the next group of the two door thing and watched them take off. Smelling our burgers gave them a sense of urgency. We took our food up to our rooms and began eating our non-hotel bounty. I had traveled in enough countries by this time to know something about foreign-made American food tastes different than how it would at home. I don't know if it's the condiments, the onions, the meat, or maybe all of the above, but it never tastes like it does when you order it on American soil.

It's a little of a disappointment.

You've built up this thing in your mind, and you take that first bite and your brain instantly registers *wrong.* You try to convince yourself that everything is okay, that it's just their way of making this, but it's too late. You eat the rest of the food knowing that somehow, you've been swindled. It's better than hotel food, but not the good 'ole USA food you had hoped for. When you're on vacation, you chalk it up to, "I went somewhere different to experience the differences", but when you're forced to go somewhere, you can't rationalize it that way.

Maybe they had a Taco Bell, too.

For now, this was good enough.

Chapter 15
Fuck

The days started getting boring.

Burger King was as far as we were allowed to venture.

The pet shop got old fast.

There was nothing to do in the hotel.

Television was not an option since we didn't speak Arabic.

We discovered most of the guests in the hotel were refugees from Kuwait. We had seen quite a few young boys around the hotel and we decided to attempt to talk to a few to make contact. They didn't know much English, but between all of us, we found out their families had escaped Kuwait before Saddam could kill them. Also, they were extremely happy the Americas had arrived so they could go back to their own country soon.

This was our first real contact with anyone from these countries with whom we could have conversations. We were learning that trying to speak to a woman was completely out of the question. The adult men looked at us like we were somehow beneath them, so that left the teenage boys. Except for the strange way of dressing, they just seemed like normal kids. I wasn't sure if the Kuwaiti men had the same stick up their asses that the Saudi men seemed to have.

By day four, our routine was getting old.

Eat shitty breakfast.

Hang out at the hotel while Fox made calls to see if the Star Flight was coming, eat lunch.

Try to talk Fox into letting us go to other places.

Get shot down.

Wait until dinner.

Oh, and listen to the gentle calling to prayer before dawn, just after breakfast, around noon, around dinner time, and after dinner time. I stopped jumping out of my skin on day three, I think.

On day five, our routine was soundly broken. Fox came to give us our Star Flight update. We were hopeful, but by now, we seemed to be getting some runaround. This damn plane should be making routine trips to Riyadh, and we should have been on one of them by now. Unfortunately, the news was beyond bad. Fox even had a sad look on his sour puss of a face.

"The commander has decided that we are staying here. There was no timeline on the Star Flight, so they changed our orders to remain in Riyadh."

OH FUCK! FUCK NO! No, No, NO!

I'm pretty sure the "FUCK NOs" were coming out of every mouth in front of him. Fox continued, "We are going to be in-processed and start building a tent city at ELF-1. As soon as possible, we will move out of the hotel and into the tent city." Of course, the questions starting flying.

What will we do here?

Is Oman completely out of the picture?

How long are we staying?

When the questions began to tail off, he began to tell us some answers. Until we get fire trucks, we will be building the tent city so all the incoming troops have somewhere to live. Oman is not an option anymore. Someone else will be sent there, but it will not be us. We will stay here until we go home.

Yup.

Fuck, and not in a fun "condom" kind of way. Ugh.

Chapter 16
LOCAL CUSTOMS

Now that it was determined we were staying, we had to officially *in process*. We had to learn about Saudi Arabia, their customs, and what was expected of us while we were "guests" in this fair land. For instance, we were to not, under any circumstances, to attempt to meet and or hook up with any of the local girls/women.

Zero.

Nada.

Hands Off.

We ain't kidding.

That shit could cause an international situation, so steer clear.

We were told about some of their laws, especially ones concerning their religions and that we were likely to accidentally break if we didn't know better.

If you have a Christian bible, hide that thing.

If you are Jewish and wear a necklace proclaiming your Jewishness, hide that thing.

Not being very religious, I wasn't overly offended, but I could understand how a person could be.

Weren't we saving this country's ass from being invaded? They didn't sound very appreciative, did they?

Also, believe it or not, they apparently didn't take kindly to stealing or adultery. You could lose a hand if you did one, and your life (if you were a woman) if you did the other. They would carry out these sentences in a very public way, just to let everyone know they weren't messing around. They had a large public square the American's called "chop chop square." Every Sunday, you could go down to the square and witness hands being lopped off and women being stoned to death, or in some cases a good old school beheading. Soon after the Americans starting arriving in large numbers, they shut down this Sunday sentencing because of the extra large crowds. Apparently, the Americans wanted to see some good 'ole fashion capital punishment in action. They didn't start this back up until after we left several months later. The backlog must have been a bloodbath.

Another "no-no" was sitting in a way with your legs crossed that showed the bottom of your shoe or foot. This was akin to telling someone they are "lower than the dirt beneath my foot." It only got weirder.

Some of the ickier customs were the ones concerning how men treated young boys and other men. We witnessed older men holding hands with young boys in public, and not in a fatherly way. It was downright fucking creepy.

We made friends with some Saudi Firefighters eventually, and they let us know that Saudi society sees women as a way to make babies, and boys/men as ways to have fun.

That took a long-ass time to wrap our heads around.

Every time we were in public and saw the men/boy hand-holding, it took a good deal of self-control to not acknowledge the disgustingness of it in some way. Telling yourself that different cultures had different ways of life just didn't cut it. Man, I hoped we didn't have to stay in this fucked up country very long.

Besides customs, we were given information on how to receive mail, where to get our guns if we were ever attacked, and a tour of the rest of ELF1, which was extremely short because the compound was so small. However, the most interesting stop was the wood shop. The guys in charge of it were good 'ole boys who seemed to like the firemen and wanted to make our lives easier. They told us that we had unlimited use of their wood and equipment, so if we needed to make something, feel free to come make it. We made good on this offer, very soon.

.

Chapter 17
UnCIVIL ENGINEER

The military likes to have several job titles fall under a category umbrella. For instance, firefighters were lucky enough to fall under the category of civil engineering. Until this point in my Air Force career, all that meant was that I had an extra patch on my uniform. The sad reality was, I really had very little idea what a civil engineer was but I was about to find out.

Without the ability for firemen to actually fight fires, we became manual laborers. If something needed lifted, moved, or built, it was our job to lift, move, or build it. Welcome to the military.

Welcome to the last few months of the Air Force. Aim High.

This was starting to feel like the 1981 movie *Stripes*. Fox was Sgt. Hulka and the rest of the cast were yet to be named, although I was actually aiming more for the Hawkeye character from M*A*S*H.

We were trucked to a sand field next to ELF1 and told this is where the tent city would be built. First, we were to build a few actual tents for the latrine (bathroom), the mess hall (cafeteria), and MWR (Morale, Welfare and Recreation). They were honest-to-God tents: canvas, poles, and ropes. Tents. The latrine one was the most important. These tents come as kits; you build the outside and then the inside. There were toilet stalls and areas to collect the poop and also a large bladder that contained water for people to shower and wash their hands. The bladder (seems like an appropriate name for what its job was) looked like a black, rubber, super oversized hot tub and could hold hundreds of gallons of water. If you were a person with an imagination, you could conceivably invent other uses for this item. Conceivably. In fact, if you put your mind to it, you could do that with several procured pieces of inventory and equipment. *Some people* have a gift for this type of thinking.

Jonesy showing off our latrine building skills.

When you are in Saudi Arabia, you learn something real fucking quick: if it is metal, and the sun is shining, that metal is hot. Real hot. So fucking hot that if you pick it up without gloves, you only do that shit once, because now you probably have some blisters. The tent poles were metal so we were each issued a thick pair of leather work gloves. Armored with sunglasses, hats, and gloves but our uniform shirts off, we began building these tents.

We would work thirty minutes, and then get a 15-minute break to stand in the MWR tent with a big-ass fan blowing on us. In the beginning, before anything was built, our breaks consisted of jumping back in the truck and cooling off in the air conditioning. To prevent us from shriveling up immediately or bursting into flames, we were told to keep at least one bottle of water with us at all times. We were given access to unlimited amounts of 1.5-liter bottles of water and most of us kept one in each pocket of our BDU pants. We were constantly told to drink since Americans were dropping like flies from the heat and dehydration.

I could believe it.

The heat from the sun hitting exposed skin felt more like radiation burns than heat from the sun back home. It was heat and sunlight like I'd never experienced. By the time our thirty minutes were up, we were all ready to leap into the truck. Getting out after fifteen minutes became more like twenty and twenty-five minutes sometimes.

Where was my Oman beach?!?

Chapter 18
Monkeys and Accordions

While we were busy constructing tents, shipments of giant square boxes starting arriving. The boxes were about seven feet high and ten feet wide, about five feet deep from front to back. But these were *magic* boxes, at least in the sense that what you were seeing was not what you were seeing. The front of the box had a door and two windows, as did the back of the box. Ready for the magic? If you took the front and back of the box and pulled them apart, the entire box expanded to around eighteen feet long, and the parts that expanded away from the center looked just like an accordion. This was a new kind of "tent" shelter. The front and back were solid. The middle section that everything expanded away from was hard around the outside and had hookups for electricity, heat, and air conditioning. Floors were dropped in, lights were added inside, and prest-o, change-o, you had a place to live after you added some nifty cots. This was our life for the next few weeks.

Build expandable tent shelters, day and night, working in shifts. Hundreds of them.

Neatly made rows and columns of expandable tents, for as far as the eye could see.

As soon as the first couple expandable tents were made, we moved out of The White Palace Hotel, and directly into the brand new (still had that *new tent smell*) tents. To be comfortable, each one fit six people to leave room between the cots for makeshift shelves (we made ours from boxes and duct tape), as well a table and chair. We could also store our bags. Soon, however, we learned there was something wrong with the environmental system of our expandable. The adjustment for temperature was broke, so it stayed on "iceberg" setting all of the time. We would be near-

Tent after expanded. Jonesy.

freezing inside and step outside to be blasted by desert heat in the 120s. Just to sleep, we had to zip our sleeping bags so only our faces were exposed. It was hilarious and stupid at the same time. We looked like pickles with faces.

After a few weeks of crazy-ass building, we were minding our own business, putting together what seemed to be our one-millionth tent. We had our shirts off, a nifty, just issued scarf around our necks, and rocking our Ray Ban sunglasses. Hey, if you had to work in these conditions, you might as well get a tan and look good doing it. It was at that exact time that some pissy-ass General drove by and witnessed the abomination of our naked arms. We had apparently just committed the worst act of heresy since Judas pocketed the silver. He had his driver (Generals don't drive themselves, for God's sake!) immediately stop so he could track down Fox and read him the riot act. We were to *immediately* get the scarves off, put our uniform shirts on and work five times harder (okay, I made up the "work harder" bit, but you see where I'm going here).

The General got back in his air-conditioned, driver-driven, flag-waving car and scurried off to do more important General work.

Fox, red-faced and looking pissed off, as usual, rounded us up to tell us the news. Our response was pretty universal, WHAT THE FUCK?!

Really?!

Does this asswipe know we are working in a fucking desert, where it's 128 degrees in the shade?!

Our answer to this was to take much longer breaks and work much less.

Isn't the military wonderful?

The monkeys continued their accordion dance.

Chapter 19
The British Are Coming!
Thank GOD!

The first time Americans heard, "The British are coming!" we got a bit upset. Horses were ridden, pitchforks were obtained, rifles were loaded. Time to send those Brits marching home, maybe with a few extra holes. Since then, we've buried the hatchet, shared some cocktails, and fought a few wars together. We've gone from fighting the royals to getting up in the middle of the night to watch them get married. We've, metaphorically, kissed and made up with our British ancestors and were thrilled to hear the British were coming this again.

Fox and Cowboy made friends with some guys who worked as contractors from British Aerospace. Did I happen to mention that Saudi Arabia is a "dry" country? No alcohol.

None.

Nada.

You are forbidden to partake, import, or otherwise be in possession of such liquids.

Yes, buggery is fine, but keep the spirits outside the borders.

When the Saudis hire companies to work in their country, they don't let them live in the general population. They put them in a "compound". It really is exactly how it sounds. It's a walled and gated community that only people from each country live in. In this case, it was the "British Compound", and because the Saudi people didn't come into their compound, well, what happens in Vegas stays in Vegas (or, in this case, what happens in the British Compound stays in the British Compound.)

The British are smart and crafty people. It's only luck that we Americans aren't still English subjects. One of our new British friends, Bill, invited Fox and Cow to the "compound". Being nice Americans, they accepted the offer, and on one of their days off, took a little trip. The Brit Compound was in a part of the city of Riyadh itself.

The rest of us had no idea that they were making this trip. I'm not sure if the Brits told them to keep this on the *down low,* or they decided this for themselves. Once they were inside, they were ushered up to what can only be described as a proper British Pub and served a pint of actual beer. Now, imagine that for about a month, none of us had had one ounce, one drop, one whiff of an alcoholic beverage. I wasn't there, but I can only imagine the look these guys must have had when the official pint glasses were handed to them. It must have been like being in Disney World when you are five years old, and Mickey Mouse walks up, swoops you into his arms, whisks you into Cinderella's Castle, and every princess gives you a kiss on the cheek. I'm not sure how many pints they had that day, but as a parting gift, Bill gave Fox a few bottles of wine to share with his friends back at the mean 'ole base. Life was about to change, and not for the worse.

Finally.

Chapter 20
Life Sucks Less

Upon their arrival back at the expandable land of Oz, I could tell Fox was torn. It was obvious he had something to tell us but was trying to figure out when, or even if, he should. I suppose he knew he couldn't keep this to himself for very long, but what I really imagined, much later, was that he wanted to keep the parting gifts all for himself as his own private stash.

Why?

Because deep down inside, Fox was a dick (well, on the surface too).

If he could keep this pub and those bottles of wine a secret, he would have. Thankfully, Cowboy would *never* have done that. We had a little secret get-together inside our accordion, and Fox made a few precious bottles of wine appear like a rabbit from a top hat. It was almost as impressive as Jesus turning water into wine. Since Fox was nowhere close to Jesus, this miracle was even harder to believe. For a moment, we all just stared at the bottles, as if they couldn't possibly be the very thing that was before us.

Wine bottles?

Wine IN wine bottles?

Suddenly big smiles were everywhere, and we started asking questions. That is when I realized Fox wanted this all for himself. He said these were *his* friends, and he didn't know if he could get any more. He didn't even tell us about the bar, just that it had come from his British friends. For a while, no one pressed this issue. We had cups to find and wine to drink.

The first small glass was an ass-kicker. Nice, dark purple and strong. The boozy smell hit your nose before the liquid hit your lips, signaling what was to come. It was just what the doctor ordered. I could feel that wonderful burn all the way to my liver. WOW!

Before long, all the bottles were empty and we had to hide the evidence. We couldn't just leave wine bottles in a trash area that someone might happen upon. If our asses got reamed for not wearing shirts while making tents in the desert heat, imagine what hole we would be dropped in if this little international incident was discovered?

We eventually decided on burying the bottles inside three different layers of trash.

Once we literally buried the evidence, the question portion of the day began. Where exactly did this come from?

How and when do we get more?

Where do these people live?

When can we go there? (yeah, we asked that question a few times)

Eventually, it was Cowboy who came to the rescue. Cow could make friends with anyone, which came in handy more than once. His southern charm knew no limits. I'm sure Bill and Hillary (the British couple, not the Clintons) could see right through Fox (he wasn't exactly a tough book to read) but Cowboy came across as a genuinely nice guy that instantly made you smile. Although he was able to tell us about his British adventure, he couldn't promise any further wine or contact as well, since Bill didn't offer, yet, and Fox and Cowboy were either too polite or tanked to ask. Either way, we seemed to have a foot in the door, and that was better than a foot in the ass. Plans needed to be discussed and made because this went quickly from accordion living sucksville to the Isle of Hope and Promise.

Chapter 21
We Be Firemen…..Kind Of

The tent-building gig was getting old. There were firemen back at the flight line, but they were contracted firemen from the Philippines. We told Fox he should make the argument that since there were American Air Force aircraft flying in and out, there should be American firemen, too. But we had a problem.

We didn't have any fire trucks and being on the bucket brigade really wasn't a good argument.

Apparently, the people with the big brains agreed with us for once and came up with a unique solution. Until we were able to acquire our own fire trucks, we would share the Filipino's trucks.

Okay. Sure. Whatever turned us back into firemen was better than being a full-time tent builder.

At first, we had shifts. Some of us would continue as tent builders because we now knew how to do it and were good at it. Others would become firemen again. Our first order of business was to learn how to drive and operate a fire truck from the Philippines. You would think if you've met one fire truck, you've met them all.

They all shoot water and drive, right?

Big wrong.

To begin with, Filipino people are much shorter than your average American, and they built these trucks to reflect that fact. The first time we climbed into the cab of their big blue truck and tried to sit down, every single one of us whacked our knees into the dashboard. It was a quick and painful lesson. We weren't even in our bunker gear (fireman's term for the protective clothing they wear to fight fires).

All of the numerous buttons in the cab, the ones that started the truck and turned on the water and foam and hoses, were all in a different language. Awesome. We had to learn the capacities and tolerances of this particular truck.

How much water and foam did it hold?

What else could it do, or not do?

Even with all of these little challenges, it was better than being a tent builder. Within a few days, we had learned enough about the truck to operate it, and a work schedule was put together. We were firemen again!

Only pic of weird fire truck from Philippines. Notice the steering wheel in the middle and crazy hatches on top.

It was around this same time that we were offered a second fire truck, a structural pumper (made to put out building fires, not aircraft). It looked like it came right off the 1962 assembly line. Some would describe it as a *classic*. It was almost museum-worthy, but at the end of the day, it was a fire truck. Sure, it leaked water and drove slow, but a truck is a truck. A lovely dark blue color, it was assigned as tent city's fire truck. One of the accordion tents

was turned into a makeshift fire department. Now we had two fire departments. One on the flight line (airport) and one at the tents.
 Hot damn! Suck it Civil Engineers! Time to tear that stupid patch off!

'Ole blue at Tent City Fire Department.

Inside the Tent City Fire Dept.

Dunc on the phone at Tent City Fire Dept (expandable tent)

Chapter 22
Vacation in Hell

Things began to get a little better. We were on a regular fireman's work schedule, that is, twenty-four hours work, twenty-four hours off. There was talk of a "kelly day" in the future. A "kelly day" is a fireman's extra day off, every other week. For instance, you pick Wednesday, and you never work Wednesdays anymore, which means every other week, you get a three-day break. It's a bone they throw to having to work the twenty-four on/off schedule. If you work the system and put a vacation day on either side of a three-day break, you end up with some good vacation days without burning up actual vacation time. Some people know how to work the system; some stay oblivious to it their entire military career.

Work days began to look a bit more like actual Air Force firefighter days. We got into a routine.

Come to work at 7am, have roll call, get assigned to a truck (we only had the one for now), check out the truck (gas, oil, radiator fluid, water, foam, lights, siren, radios, yadda, yadda), and then do some training.

Each day we would pick a topic or thing that needed to be trained on so we stayed current on our skills. Rope tying, or how a particular truck operates, or rescue skills, or aircraft familiarization. There are countless topics to choose from.

After a morning training session, lunch became the next priority. A chow hall had been set up for everyone at ELF1, since new people were arriving every day. Unfortunately, the chow hall was manned mostly by non-Americans for now, which in itself wasn't a bad thing, except they were also serving us local food that they tried to turn into American food.

They were not successful.

They meant well, but on most days, I had no idea what I was actually eating. Around 11am, we would send one or two guys in a truck to the

Typical Training Report. Cowboy gave a class on how to use Gas Mask.

chow hall, since we couldn't exactly drive a fire truck there. They would pick up enough "take out" orders for all of the guys working, and bring them back. We would open our lunches (or dinners, it was the same process twice a day), and take the next five minutes discussing among ourselves what we thought the meat was made of, or what kind of other weird shit we were looking at. This went on for several weeks, until the food shipments caught up with the troops, and we were able to eat mostly American food again.

Up to this point, Fox was in charge. We kept our entire work schedule very simple, sprinkled with some common sense. We realized we weren't in the USA anymore, so anything that pertained

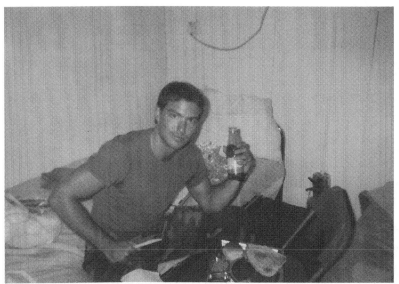

Trying new and exciting local food. My bunk at the fire department.

to firefighting back home was put on the back burner, or just eliminated. We didn't have to maintain hydrants or do inspections. Even small shit like washing trucks, which is a mainstay in a fire department, was eliminated.

Why?

We were in a desert, in a pre-war condition. The trucks didn't really get dirty and if they did, big deal. Yep, for about a month, things ran easy and smooth, but nothing that good can last for long.

Chapter 23
Invitation ONLY

As things settled into a routine, Fox and Cowboy were able to get a few of us invited to the British Compound, which really meant, we were going to THE PUB! All of us who were off-shift made our way to the compound. It was weird to see the high walls and gate that surrounded the housing area where the British people lived.

What a strange way to live.

I didn't have long to ponder this situation since we were hot and heavy to see where the beverage drinking took place. Through a door and up some stairs, a familiar smell greeted me before I entered the room.

Beer.

That smell you get about half a step before entering a bar.

A smell so ingrained into the essence of the molecules around you that it will be there ten years after the earth is destroyed.

Your brain registers the smell and the smile appears on your face without your knowledge.

One minute you are on some weird street in Saudi Arabia, the next minute you are in a British compound, and the next, you are in a secret English Pub. Dartboard on the wall.

Cricket bats.

Bar with real bar towels.

Wood. Pint glasses. Stools. Tables.

It was as if we were instantly transported to our friendly neighbor's island thousands of miles away. This can fuck with a person's head if one were inclined to let such things bother them. But when a guy hands you a big frosty beer in a pint glass, you just say, "thank you." Then you smile and tip that brew back. I wasn't sure how they pulled this minor miracle off, but it was giving me some ideas. Time for ideas later; now it was time to see if I could drink my bodyweight in beer.

As we sat there, enjoying the spirits and our friends, we discovered how this all came to be. The British, as well as many other countries, had been working as contractors in Saudi Arabia for a very long time. As more and more people showed up, each country of people was put into their own areas, so they could be themselves, and the local people wouldn't have to be subjected and offended by the godless (Allahless?) customs of outsiders.

Who could blame them? How could we expect them to be assaulted by a woman's bare exposed shoulder, or her legs or, Allah forbid, her actual face. These atrocities must be kept behind walls and gates, and so the compounds came into existence. After the walls were built, and the gates firmly in place, our British friends decided to bring a little hometown delight to their surroundings. Thus, the pub was born, and slowly, over time, people brought bits of home to make it so authentic, you'd never know you weren't actually in jolly 'ole England.

This arrangement with our new friends didn't last for as long as we would have liked. After about our third visit to this oasis, they figured out that we were drinking their stash faster than they could resupply themselves. They kindly told us we were cut off, but not completely. This dark cloud had the most sparkly of silver linings. Instead of showing us the door, they told us the secrets of the universe, they gave us the recipe for making WINE! It was the single biggest turning point in the war for us. There would be BEFORE THE KNOWLEDGE and AFTER THE KNOWLEDGE. Things were about to change. Our lives were about to transform in ways we couldn't begin to fathom or understand. I can easily say that I wouldn't be married to the person I am today, and not have the kids I have today without this single event. But let's not get ahead of ourselves, because life moved fast here, and you had to be ready to adapt on a dime.

Chapter 24
Set your watch to the year 1943

There was a rumor one of the commercial pilots announced, "Set your watch to the year 1943," as he was landing in Riyadh. When he stepped off the plane, he was promptly told he was not welcome in the Kingdom of Saudi Arabia again.
The truth must have stung a bit to the locals who were riding the metal bird that day.

It wasn't long after our arrival that we were told to visit the *Batha*. If we were looking for some great shopping from the local people, this was the place to go. The adventure seekers like myself decided to see what this was all about so we made our way to the center of Riyadh to experience what it was like to travel in a time machine to a place where time hasn't moved for two thousand years.

You really don't see or understand what you are entering until you are already inside of it.

From the outside, it seems like you are just entering an alley-sized street for foot traffic only, but once inside, you've just been enveloped into a labyrinth of twisting and intersecting alleys with no listed names or signs to identify where you are.

This is all within several blocks, and to a casual or first-time shopper, it's easy to get lost. Overhead, the alleys are covered by fabrics, so the desert sun doesn't consume those inside, which keeps the environment in continuous shadow. The walls of the alleys are clay or stone; each shop has its large, wooden doors wide open with their wares pouring into the alley. The aroma of incense is almost overwhelming, leaving a light haze hanging in the air. As you look in the shops, it seems most of the items being sold come from ancient tombs.

This wasn't 1990 anymore.

Whether the items were authentic or just made to look old, it felt as if we had just stepped into the movie set for *Indiana Jones* at the market.

One overwhelming item sold at the Batha was gold.

Lots and lots of gold.

Not your typical USA gold, this was *Saudi* gold.

As I looked at the tables and tables of gold everywhere, I was struck by how the color was so different from the gold back home. After a quick examination, we discovered that this gold was a much higher karat than what American sellers display. This was all 18-24 karat gold, and it looked amazing. What was more amazing was how cheap it was.

Note to self: *Invest in gold next time I'm in the Middle East.*

Live and learn.

Now came the fun. It took us about ten seconds to learn that you don't just *buy* something at the Batha, you haggle for everything. Men with hands full of items will accost you as you walk by, using the few words of English they have memorized.

"Special price for Americans"!

Yeah, special price, my ass.

The *special price* was probably ten times the local price.

At first it took us a while to convert the prices in our heads, but eventually, we got the hang of it, and what was surprising was that most of the time, the prices they were asking was already dirt cheap. That didn't stop us from trying to haggle the price down even more. It was almost like a stage show every time we showed interest in an item.

The shopkeeper would name some price.

We would act offended that they would think we were stupid Americans who would pay such an outrageous price.

We'd say some crazy low number.

They would act offended because now they were losing money on the deal. We would begin to walk away and they would yell another amount, usually adding, "Because you are American, I give you special price!"

Man, we must have heard that a thousand times before we left many months later, but it never got old and always made me laugh.

I loved this new way of shopping, and only a few times did I feel like I lost the deal. I ended up with plenty of momentos and awesome memories. Many months later, when I returned home, it took a long time to realize I couldn't haggle for items at the mall or other shops.

Shopping in America is boring.

One of the most overwhelming aspects of this culture was also on display at the Batha. As we strolled through the allies, merrily buying and bartering, the loudspeakers swiftly announced *call to prayer*, at which time the shopkeepers made their way to the nearest mosque. If there were tables with merchandise in the alley, the shopkeeper would just take a piece of fabric and lay it over the table, then leave. There could be tens of thousands of dollars in gold on the table, it didn't matter.

I was stunned.

How were thieves not pushing wheelbarrows down the middle of the lane, just scooping up loads of merchandise and running off?

We asked one of our Saudi friends later, and he explained that in Saudi, justice was swift, and punishment was severe.

If someone steals and is caught, they lose a hand in "chop chop square" on the next Sunday. No appeals.

Wham. Bam. No hand, Sam.

There were religious police roaming the streets as well during the call to make sure you got your ass to the mosque and no laws were broken. They wielded long, heavy sticks to whack people with if they didn't seem to be moving in the right direction quickly enough. They tried to pull that shit on the Americans soon after we arrived, but we quickly, and probably somewhat aggressively, reminded them we were Americans and didn't do that. They were not amused, but before we took away their stick to shove up their ass, they got the idea.

Life here wasn't even close to Kansas and Toto was nowhere to be found.

Chapter 25
USMTM = OASIS

It was around this time that we found the best military oasis in Saudi Arabia. USMTM, which we pronounced as (You - Sah - Mitt - MMMMM). Honestly, as long as I was there, I really didn't know what the acronym stood for, but if you're the curious type it stands for United States Military Training Mission.

But what it *really* means is "place with swimming pool and awesome chow hall."

It's a small compound where the full-time American military stationed in Riyadh live and work. During our first visit, we discovered that not only was the chow hall amazing, with real food, but there happened to be a rather large swimming pool on the grounds. As firemen, we are *very* astute about opportunities. Because our military IDs got us through the front door, and because no one told us we were not allowed to use the pool, well, we used the pool.

For the first month or so, this was a highly guarded secret. There were very few military people yet to make their way to Riyadh, so we were the first to discover many little details, such as pools and British Pubs. Swimwear was quickly acquired and our new lifestyles were adapted.

This was before our winemaking skills were in full swing yet, so all of our off-time was spent poolside: working on the best tan ever, playing pool volleyball, taking a break when lunchtime rolled around and we could be assured of actual food and not some middle eastern version inside a tent.

This was our life for several weeks. Work one day, be at the pool the next. Maybe throw in a few hours at the Batha.

This didn't suck nearly as bad as the brochure suggested.

Then a girl showed up.

USMTM Pool. Note...nary a girl. Sausage Fest 1990. Ugh.

Up to this point, we really hadn't seen many females, military or otherwise, except for pre-teen Saudi girls, who apparently didn't have to wear the full black garb (affectionately referred to as "raisinets"). But one day, a tall, tan, pink bikini-clad girl walked into the pool area.

You would have thought an alien from another universe had just landed.

Eyes popped out of heads like some cartoon.

If one were to stop looking at the girl for ten seconds and watch the twenty or thirty guys, you would have seen all heads slowly swivel left and right as this girl moved around the pool.

It was funny, it was weird, it was hilarious.

A few brave guys immediately pounced on her for attention. Judging from her bikini, I believe she knew what affect she would have on the pool-goers.

After she made an appearance, other girls (okay, women), began to filter into the pre-war city, and the earth was about to take another great shift on its axis.

One lunchtime at USMTM, I grabbed my tray to stand in line for the food, but something suddenly seemed *off*.

There were linen napkins instead of paper.

The table clothes looked completely new, like someone had just opened them for the first time.

When I looked down at the first item to serve myself, I found I was staring at a big, fat, juicy steak. Like, steak from *America*.

Next to the steak was a big, fucking baked potato.

On and on the awesome food appeared down the line.

USMTM usually had good food, but this was *crazy* good food. I didn't question the bounty, I just went with it. If I said something out loud, maybe someone would tell me to leave, so I just piled up my plate and kept moving.

Suddenly a large, official group descended into the chow hall. Some of them looked like scary, trained killers. One guy stood taller than the rest and had an air about him that was larger than life.

I had seen this guy on television.

Seven feet away from me was General Storm'n Norman Schwarzkopf.

Holy fuck!

This was the man running the war.

It then struck me why I was now eating so well. You don't put out cheeseburgers and fries for *The General*. And if the General is eating good, then by God, so is everyone. Woot! Woot!

Some days were certainly better than others.

Chapter 26
The Secret Recipe

Want to know how to make wine in the desert? So did everyone else.

Want to know who knew the secret recipe? A very, very, very few firemen.

The Coca-Cola recipe was guarded with less enthusiasm than our recipe.

Why?

First, this knowledge was illegal.

Second, if you took this knowledge and actually acted on it (i.e., make the wine), you could get kicked out of the military, kicked out of the country, and/or go to jail. Maybe all of the above, in no particular order.

Lastly, being the sole makers (and later distributors) of alcohol gave us several advantages above and beyond our other brothers-in-arms. The repercussions if discovered were mind-boggling, and none of us were excited to find out the many ways the military would punish us if we got caught. But even that threat didn't stop us from becoming wartime vintners.

Desperate times call for desperate measures and we were fucking desperate.

Just having the recipe wasn't enough. For a normal operation, you needed special equipment. Sanitizing liquid, containers to ferment, bottles, yadda, yadda, yadda. We would need to buy the actual stuff to make the wine. Since we didn't have access to a local vineyard for grapes, we were using the British Plan B method.

The recipe was simple: grape juice, sugar, water, and finally, the magic ingredient, yeast. We found a local grocery store on the outskirts of Riyadh to acquire our goodies. We decided if one of us were to buy all of these things together, we might draw attention to ourselves, so we separately bought the ingredients.

I'd buy the juice, Dunc got the sugar, Cowboy the yeast.

We even used different checkout lines, just in case. We couldn't be careful enough. I couldn't believe they didn't know what we were up to.

Who the hell buys four cases of grape juice at a time?

They kept this stuff in huge supplies, so maybe there was more of this underground movement going on than met the eye.

Hmmmm.

But where were we going to ferment our concoction? We needed something that didn't scream, *"Home brewing taking place here!"*

I came up with the perfect solution.

My dad made home brew wine when I was a kid growing up, so I knew that whatever we put this liquid gold into, it needed to be able to vent the carbon dioxide gas that the yeast critters farted as they ate the sugar. My solution was to use the five-gallon gas containers. They had big openings to pour our ingredients into and a small relief valve on top. They were practically *made* for this project. The only drawback was the relief valve would have to be manually opened once a day to let the pressure out, but that wasn't a big deal to those motivated to have some booze.

Finally, we needed somewhere to hide these containers while they turned juice into wine. We were living in the expandable tents; having five-gallon gas cans inside looked pretty suspicious. We were coming up with all kinds of crazy ideas of where to put them.

Bury them? No, that was too much work to dig them up so often.

Keep them in the Fire Department? Hell no! Too easy for someone to find and or steal.

The answer finally came when we remembered our tour of ELF1 soon after we arrived. Our friends who ran the wood shop said we were welcome to use their tools and as much wood as we wanted anytime.

So we built a box. I think it was Cowboy who actually built it. It was big enough to fit several five-gallon containers inside. When closed, it looked like we just built a bed stand with storage space. *Genius!*

The day finally came when we added all of the ingredients together, closed up the jugs, and waited. We were told when the mixture stopped giving off gas in a few weeks, it was drinkable wine.

That sounded a bit too easy, but who was I to argue with science?

Mix stuff, wait, drink.

What could be simpler? It wasn't exactly that simple, but we learned as we went. Nothing exploded and no one died. By those standards, it was a success. Eventually.

Chapter 27
Making Friends

Around this time, we started making good friends with a couple of our Saudi firemen. Cowboy and Dunc went out of their way to get to know Saud and Akmed.

I'm not sure who they were actually more interested in: their new, American firemen friends or the girls that came to visit their new, American firemen friends. Maybe it was the girls.

More on the girls later, but suffice it to say, our Saudi firemen buddies had overwhelming reactions when women showed up.

As happy as we were to have girls hanging around with us, these guys were so over-the-top-excited it was impossible for them to stop smiling constantly. Imagine growing up in a society where, as a kid, you got to see and play with girls and boys your own age, just like most places on planet Earth. But around the time boys and girls started noticing each other in *special* ways, someone throws a black sack over the girl and no one but her family is allowed to see her again. She must wear the black sack outside at all times.

I hate to judge other cultures, but in this case I will: it's fucking crazy.

The only way you get to see your poor childhood friend again is if you pony up thirty goats, two double humpers, and some cash to buy her for marriage one day. Seeing only your mom and sisters until you're married has got to screw with you. Hence the creepy "man-boy" hookups we kept witnessing?

We would be at the fire department working and the Saudi guys would blatantly ask, "Are the girls coming today?"

There aren't words to describe how sad they looked when we had to tell them *no* sometimes. What a crazy country.

It was fun talking to these guys. They seemed to have some interest in our culture and we were having fun learning about theirs.

At first, we wanted to learn as many curse words in Arabic as they could teach us, because hey, we're Americans, that's what we do.

"Hey Saud. How do you say *fuck me running* in Arabic"?

He would tell us, and we would butcher it badly, but finally, he'd sound it out so we could say the words, "Neck, Knee, Jeddy".

I have no idea if we were saying the right thing, but it was fun.

Every time I wanted to call home from the shitty little fire department phone, I'd have to call the base operator, who spoke no English and ask "for an outside line".

Saud hooked me up with, "Men-fah, lick hut", except the "hut" part was more of a guttural spit wad sound in the back of your throat.

The operator guy didn't like my accent apparently the first few times, but I wasn't playing his game.

He'd say back "Men fah lick hut?" but in some shitty way that implied I was an idiot.

See what you can infer from just someone's tone, regardless of the language? Maybe I was reading into it.

I'd reply, "Yeah, mother fucker, Men Fah Lick HUT! Now give me an outside line!"

He'd hang up on me sometimes, but I'd just call back. Sometimes it was funny, sometimes I wanted to kick his ass.

We'd learn other words that could get us some food, or *thank you*. Nothing too complicated. We were Americans, after all, and since we were saving their asses, they should be learning English, right?

Wrong.

We would half-jokingly tell Saud and Ahmed that they should be happy our American asses were there protecting their sad, oil-rich asses, or Saddam Fucking Hussein would be rolling over their houses and raping their women, or men, or goats.

Whatever Saddam fucked. It was a subject worthy of debate. I digress.

But apparently, Saud's god, Allah, gave them a different point of view. No matter how good, or bad something was, it was, "the will of Allah." So if Saddam invaded Saudi Arabia, took their oil, raped their goats, and stole their women, well, it was simply, "the will of Allah." I'm no theologian or priest, or Vulcan, but at the time, this entire, "will of Allah" thing seemed like a giant pile of steaming horse crap (probably camel crap).

Good Lord! We were risking our lives to save their stupid oil, I mean country, at least show a little thanks or goodwill or slap a brother a high five or some shit, but geeeeeez us!

(FYI, no Jesus references allowed in Saudi Arabia) Hmmmm. Maybe they were right in the end, but who can know?

Chapter 28
The Pros from Dover....or Langley, or Somewhere

We got into a routine. Fox made schedules, we worked shifts, shit got built, fire departments were shaping up. We even had the promise of some vino on the way. Then someone else showed up.

Dammit.

A whole platoon of new firemen suddenly appeared one day out of the fucking mist. In a single day, we went from Fox, who we were able to manage in our own way, to a group of guys we knew nothing about other than several of them outranked Fox. He went from being *Top Dog* to *Dog Shit* in the matter of three camel winks and a goat burp. Actually, it was a mixture of funny and sad to see the look on his face when he realized he was now barely better than the rest of us. But what we also found out is that we went from an idiot leader to a psychopathic leader as fast as a camel fart in the desert breeze.

The Air Force found a pile of petrified dinosaur shit on one of their bases. They dug it up and found Master Sergeant Tribuck underneath, ready to kick ass and take names. The problem was, Tribuck had been around since Moses parted the sea, and being that old made you cranky and set in your ways. But he was sure of one thing when he stepped off the plane and into the desert heat of Saudi Arabia. Whoever was in charge here already, and whatever they were doing, it was wrong. But he would fix it. It was time to get this train back on the track and turn this cluster fuck into a real man's fire department. He made all of these decisions before he took his third step off the plane. Tribuck (eventually just known as BUCK), was a short shit of a man. Stout, short crew cut hair, little mustache. He was some version of Jackie Gleason from Smokey and the Bandit. He always looked pissed off, but if I had a stick that big up my ass all the time, I'd be pissed off too.

As soon as he walked in the door, he immediately made Fox, as well as the rest of us, aware that there was a new sheriff in town, and his name was Tribuck. He immediately put his people in charge of everything. New assistant chiefs for each shift, new shifts, new everything. Personally, I wasn't in charge of jack shit to begin with, so I went from being mid-totem pole to lower-mid totem pole, which was just hunky dory with me. The less responsibility, the better. Unfortunately, my crystal ball was on the fritz, because there was some shit coming down the pike that I couldn't imagine in a lifetime. Now it was time to meet the new guys, find out who was cool and who the idiots were, and deal with whatever came next. Why can't we just leave the apple cart alone?

Chapter 29
Trucks

Around the same time the new dudes showed up, we also acquired American fire trucks. We had been sharing this Filipino truck for weeks, but it was so comically small for most Americans it was laughable. Squishing ourselves into the cab sideways was getting old. One morning we arrived for work and were greeted by a sand-colored P-19. At the time, the P-19 was one of the newest crash fire trucks used by the USAF.

The overwhelmingly best part of this sleek, fast truck is that it actually had air conditioning.

We were told there were all kinds of American military vehicles buried in the Saudi desert, just waiting to be dug up in case some shit hit the fan one day. We were also told that it had taken weeks to dig them out and then clean them up in order to transport them to areas they were needed.

It all sounded like horse shit to me, but I really didn't care where they came from. If the magical truck fairy wanted to bestow new fire trucks to us, then who was I to ask silly questions? It meant we were finally rid of those clown car fire trucks and we could once again ride and work in equipment to which we were accustomed.

Good 'ole P-19

We also received a P-4 fire truck and a rescue truck. The P-4 is a big, boxy, beast. Whoever built it had no imagination and designed it purely for function. It looks like a large, long, box on its side with wheels added. It has large water cannons on the front and on the roof. I suppose when it came out it in the mid-1970s, it was a fireman's wet dream, but by the time I saw my first one in 1989, it already looked like it needed to be retired years ago.

Maybe the military just beats the shit out of equipment.

Who knows.

This one was no different. Same desert color and it had seen better days, but it moved forward, held water and foam, and shot liquid at things on fire, so it was good enough. Even better was that the crew compartment was *huge*. You walked in on either side by way of a full-sized door. You stepped up, *without crouching over*, and walked to your seat. There were two seats up front (driver and crew chief), and two behind them (linemen), so it fit four people very comfortably. No more whacked knees.

Finally, there was the rescue truck. The truck looks like an extended cab pickup truck with front and back seats. The rear section is a large utility truck, with many doors on the sides and rear for loads of tools, stretchers, air packs, saws and other rescue equipment. The job of this three-man crew was to make entry into an aircraft, shut it down, deploy any onboard fire suppression capabilities the aircraft had, find and extract any crew or passengers, and get the hell back out in one piece.

The best part of being on a rescue crew was being pretty much in charge of yourselves. You had a smaller vehicle you could just jump into at any time, so you came and went as you pleased. If someone questioned where you were going, you just said, "training," and rarely did someone pry further. You trained on stuff the rest of the fire department usually didn't. It was a harder job, but the perks these guys got far outweighed their responsibilities, or at east that's the way it appeared from the lowly position I usually occupied.

It was of little surprise that when the new trucks showed up, Master Sergeant New Guy Tribuck installed his guys into the top positions, especially the rescue truck. A sergeant named Mike was made the crew chief, Archabold was in the back seat, and, somehow, Cowboy made it into the driver position.

We now worked the normal fireman's routine:

Come to work and have roll call.

Yesterday's shift would load onto a bus and go back to tent city.

The new shift would do their daily truck inspections and then whatever training was scheduled for the day.

Rescue guys would get in their vehicle and drive off into the abyss, not to be seen again until lunchtime or even dinner time. They were their own island, and their whereabouts usually remained a mystery.

The rest of us schleps just fell into the same routine we'd been doing stateside as firemen, and for a little while, life was *normal* again. Too normal. The *calm before the storm* normal.

Chapter 30
It Takes a War

Not long after my arrival, I started writing letters home. I'd write Martha, my mom, and my friends back home. The phone call situation, in the beginning, was ridiculous. Waiting for hours to make a six-minute phone call was nuts, so I just wrote a letter or two a day. Having loads of spare time on my hands, this seemed like a good idea. I began writing my mom and Martha about a week after I first arrived. I knew getting a letter from Saudi Arabia back to Kentucky, and then a reply back was going to take possibly weeks, but when it became obvious that I wasn't going anywhere any time soon, I started pumping out the letters. I figured it would eventually be a good way to look back and see what I was doing and thinking during my little vacation in the sand.

I wrote, and wrote, and wrote, and a few weeks later I was excited to get my first letter back. Mom had written me and told me she received my first letter. She detailed life back home and told me of all of the people supporting us.
It was good to hear from her and to know this paper was a real thing that had been in my house back home not long ago. It felt like something real, like some little safety line that I could physically feel.

A few days later, I received my second letter, again from my mom. Awesome, again! Yay, Mom! It was good to know my mail was getting home and the turnaround time was shorter than I thought it would be.

But I wondered where my mail was from Martha. Two letters from Mom, zero from my fiancée .

A couple of weeks went by, and I'd had a few more letters from Mom, still *zero* from Martha,. and zero from my friends.

I was getting a little-pissed off so I decided to call home to see what the situation was. I went to the area where they set up the phones, put my name on a list and waited a few hours until it was my turn and they called my name.

I called an operator in the United States, who connected me with an operator in my hometown, who then connected me to Martha's house.

Remember, I have a total of six minutes to use this shitty, 1948 model phone.

It was as useful as two tin cans and a string.

Every word had to be yelled.

By the time I finally heard the phone in Kentucky pick up, and the operator announced who was calling and from where, most of my time was gone.

First I spoke (yelled) to her mom that I only had a couple of more minutes, so I needed to speak with Martha. Usually, when you get on the phone, you have time to build up to the main part of the conversation. You can ask about your day or school or what's new, but time was ticking down like a missile launch here, so I had to get right to the point.

"Hello," she said.

"I've been writing to you for weeks, are you getting my letters?"

Tick. Tick. Tick.

"Martha!?"

"Yes?"

"I haven't got one letter from you yet. Are you writing?"

Silence.

Tick. Tick. Tick.

"Martha, I have less than a minute for this call. What's going on?"

Tick. Tick. Tick.

Oh man, I was about to fucking explode.

There were countless people behind me waiting to make their call. Every word I was saying could easily be heard a block away because of how loud I had to talk.

This was crazy.

"Martha, I had to wait two hours in line just to make this call, you could at least talk to me."

Nothing.

With what little dignity I could scrape off the ground, I just hung up.

Fuck this!

I left the little enclosure, not quite knowing how to feel. Is this the person I wanted to marry one day?

I could feel the stares of a hundred eyes on my back from the other people waiting their turns to scream into the shitty phones.

I had some shit to figure out. I'd write her another letter, but the next one was going to be quite different.

Chapter 31
Speaking of Letters…

Even though my lovely betrothed wasn't showering me with letters, the rest of America was on a mission. It seemed that back home, the USA was ramping up to support the troops in a big way. All kinds of campaigns were being kicked off. There was the *yellow ribbon* campaign in which people tied yellow ribbons around anything and everything.

Trees, lamp posts, stripper poles, dog tails, whatever.

Stickers were made.

Magnets passed out.

If you didn't display a yellow ribbon on something you owned, then you were clearly a communist and needed to be deported posthaste.

But the biggest campaign was the letter-writing campaign. Everyone was writing to the troops.

Churches, schools, old war heroes, and, apparently, some lonely women.

Nearly every day, during mail call, a sack of letters would get dumped on a table addressed to "Any Service Member." We were encouraged to pick one up and write back to show our thanks for supporting us. Since my dearest wasn't writing, I made up for it by writing three to five letters every day.

Some were from school kids and were very cute. They'd ask if it was hot, and sometimes if we'd killed anyone yet. Clearly, the teachers weren't reading these before the kids sent them.

Some were from vets from Vietnam. They reminded us how shitty they were treated during their war, and how determined they were to make sure that didn't happen to us this time around.

Some were from some very sympathetic people who asked if they could send us anything to make our lives easier while being gone.

Anything. Any. Thing.

Drugs.

Alcohol.

Naked pictures.

VCRs. Not VCR tapes, the actual VCR machines. Tapes, too. It was incredible.

Many of these offers were taken up. Hey, we were a bunch of dudes (mostly dudes in the beginning), sitting in the desert, little to do (yet) for entertainment, so can you blame us?

Besides the numerous pictures being sent and passed around, one nice lady started sending us bourbon balls. And she kept sending them to us. Oh man, these became very popular and so did she. She was a true American patriot. George Washington would have been proud.

Another way life is so different now from back then is the US Postal Service decided after a few weeks that postage for service people was now FREE. Yup. Instead of using a stamp, all you had to do was write the word *"free"*.

However, in the return address area, you listed your name, your wartime address, and your *Social Security Number.*

I shit you not.

Right there on the front of every letter you mailed was your social security number.

Can you imagine that today?

One day, a few months later into the war, I received a call from the post office at ELF1. It seemed that one of the nice people who worked there noticed that a package addressed to me was leaking.

Instead of ripping the package open or throwing it away, he tracked me down and gave me a call.

"Sgt. White?"

"Yep, that's me."

"This is Sgt. Postal Dude. I'd advise you to get down here immediately to pick up your package. It's leaking, and if you don't get it soon, there may not be much left of whatever it is that's inside."

"Thanks! I'll be there ASAP!"

I jumped in our little van and made my way to the mail intake area as fast as possible. It seemed that my step-dad had sent me a couple of fifths of delightful beverages. The Jack Daniels bottle had sprung a leak, probably due to some hard hits as it traveled halfway around the planet on numerous airplanes.

I arrived and found my new friend at the post office wearing a big 'ole, shit-grin on his face.

Sure enough, one side of my box was wet and had the familiar smell of Tennessee wafting from it.

"Hope you didn't lose it all," he said.

"Thanks for calling!"

I was relieved that I happened to get a sympathetic friend in the mail department, instead of some angry sergeant with a stick up his ass for rules and regulations. This could have gone sideways very fast, but instead, all was well. I took possession of my three-quarters of a bottle of Mr. Daniels, as well as an unbroken bottle of rum. Both had been packed in hollowed-out loaves of bread, but even that bit of precaution wasn't enough to completely survive the journey. You can bet that the party we had later was a doozie.

Sharing the wealth. Rum. Bucket. Kool-aid.

Chapter 32
Forgotten City

Back in 1938, Saudi Arabia discovered that under their worthless sandpit, an ocean of Texas tea (Saudi Chai?) waited to be tapped. Once the black gold started flowing, it went from a country full of sheepherders riding camels to a rich and powerful nation.

Wham. Overnight.

For many, this was a blessing from Allah. No more wandering around on smelly, humpbacked, flea-bitten ships of the desert.

No more living in tents.

As George Jefferson once said, "We're ah movin' on up"! And many did. Sheiks, and princes and kings, OH MY!

The oil flowed, the dollars (riyal) flowed and many people changed their lifestyles. They traded in their camels for Mercedes. They burned their tents and built mansions. Many thought it was for the better. Many did not.

You can take the sheepherder out of the desert, but for a great many thousands, you can't take the desert out of the sheepherder. This was a lifestyle they had been accustomed to for thousands of years. It was ingrained into the very DNA of their soul.

Ride Camel. Herd sheep. Move. Move. Move.

Always pitching the tents and pulling up stakes to move again.

Over and over and over.

For as long as they knew.

But in 1983, the government of Saudi Arabia said, "You know? We're rich. Not just rich, but *very fucking rich*. We can't have thousands of our people wandering around in the desert on smelly camels, herding their smelly goats, without any plumbing. They are shitting in the sand, not bathing often, and making us all look bad."

So, you know what the government did?

They built them an entire city. They built five bedroom houses with air conditioning and marble floors. Kitchens. Bathrooms. Running water.

They built them high-rise towers, fully furnished.

It was an enormous, honest-to-goodness, full-on city.

They rounded up the bedouins and said, "Look at this great and wonderful city for which we have spent millions upon millions upon zillions to build you! Are you not thankful that we have erected these great structures to bring you out of the desert sun and into the twentieth century?"

What could the herders say?

They looked on in amazement at this great spectacle before them and said, "Yo, bitches! We didn't *ask* you to build this city, and we ain't livin' in no freaking city! We love how we live and you can't make us stop."

They promptly jumped back on their one-humpers and went back to the lives they loved. The goats and sheep followed.

And the city, with its thousands of houses and condos and high-rise buildings, was never used. Not one person lived there. Ever.

This city in the desert did what everything else in the desert does when no one pays attention to it. It started to become buried by sand. For seventeen years the winds blew the hot sands through the streets until they disappeared. Only the tops of the houses could be seen. The high-rises stuck out as if part of a movie set for *Planet of the Apes*.

And then one day, Saddam Hussein invaded tiny Kuwait.

Suddenly, hundreds, then thousands and thousands of military people started arriving in Saudi Arabia. The poor tent city, with its hundreds of expandable tents, built by brave firemen, was about to be overwhelmed by more people than it could hold.

What to do? What to do? Hmmmmmmmm.

Then some smart man with a towel wrapped securely around his head had an epiphany.

"WAIT!" he said in his native tongue.

"I have a fucking awesome idea! Remember those stupid goat herders that refused to live in that giant city we built on the outskirts of Riyadh? Why don't we clean up Eskan (it's official name) and let all of the military people live there! Am I a genius or what?!?"

As it was written, so it was done.

Bulldozers were dispatched post-haste to scoop out the sands from the streets. Sweepers were dispatched to sweep the sand from the houses. Electricians and plumbers and others were dispatched to get shit working. And best of all, someone ordered thousands of air conditioner wall units for hot and sweaty military members to enjoy.

But these things took time.

We had time. Like the sand through the hourglass, yadda, yadda, yadda.

Then one day, while we were relaxing in our expandable habitat, Fox burst through the door with news.

"I bring forth news from THE KING!," he shouted.

Sorry, I'm getting carried away.

It was more like, "Hey, we won't have to live in these fucking tents much longer." He told us the story of the forgotten city of Eskan, and how we would be moving there in a few weeks.

Holy shit! This actually *was* some good news. He said we could take the van and drive out to look at it if we wanted and that's exactly what some of us did.

After driving through the desert for about twenty-five minutes, we found Eskan. From the side we entered, we discovered hundreds of single-story houses. All were the same color as the sand and each had a wall around it. In the distance, we could see untold numbers of high-rise towers.

We got out of the van and started walking among them. We found the front door open to one and went inside. There was no furniture, so each room was empty, but all of the floors were white marble. Each house had five bedrooms, three bathrooms, a living room, and a kitchen. There was also a separate entrance that housed a stairwell that went to the roof, so up we went. The door opened at the top to a completely flat roof that had a six-foot wall around it.

Hmmmmmm. This had some possibilities.

We looked around for a bit more and hit the road. We couldn't get out of those accordions fast enough.

Exploring Eskan for the first time. Jonesy striking a cool "Jonesy" pose.

Chapter 33
The Vino

Let's not lose track of the main topic of this adventure saga, *the wine*. Remember the wine?

We had mixed up the ingredients, put them in some brand new plastic five-gallon gas cans, and hid them in a secret box inside our expandable tent. Every day, we would have someone open the box (while using a lookout, obviously) and open the relief valve to let the carbon dioxide escape. We kept and stored all of the glass grape juice bottles because this is where the finished wine would have to be eventually put.

The bottles were actually pretty cool. Instead of having to deal with corks, the bottles had the nifty metal pieces on top that swung a stopper into place to lock it down. Easy peasy.

While our juice was slowly transforming into scarlet libations, we got word we were soon moving into Eskan. After our initial excitement, we pondered how exactly we were going to transport our mixtures from Tent City to Eskan City, without incurring prying eyes and nosy questions. It was finally decided that we would just leave it all in the box to move it. That should work. But what would we do with it once we arrived at Eskan? Hmmmm?

Moving, storing and making the wine became a game of "Where's Waldo?" Our first solution was just fucking crazy. We were off the chart paranoid. As much as all of us didn't want to be here, we sure as hell didn't want to be thrown out of the country and the Air Force for making alcohol. I *especially* didn't want to get tossed out of the military with only a couple of months left, so we ended up taking some extraordinary precautions.

Some of us went back to Eskan on a recon mission. We needed to find some secret place inside our soon-to-be house to hide our science experiment. At the time, we felt that our new houses would be subject to unannounced inspections, so we had to be ready for anything at any time. Outwardly, we would look like good 'ole, law-abiding, by the regs, military firemen. Behind the scenes, we ended up breaking every rule we heard there was to break.

Hey, boredom breeds lawlessness and our brand was something to be witnessed to believe.

Front view of Eskan house. Wall and front door. The tower is stairs to roof.

When we entered our walled and gated, soon-to-be house, we noticed a metal square on the ground before we got to the door.

Hmmmmmm? Wonder what that is?

We pried it open and looked inside.

Water. It was a huge cistern filled with hundreds of gallons of water.

Boing! Idea!!

What if....now, hang with me here....what if we took the five-gallon jugs and floated them in the cistern? Could we do that?

Nothing ventured, nothing gained.

No one in their right mind would look down there for people making homemade wine, right?

The plan was hatched.

That is exactly what we did.

Before the big move to Eskan, we began our clandestine operation. We gently loaded our wine box into the van and drove

out to our soon-to-be new house. Two of us lifted the heavy metal lid off the cistern hole. We
threw Jonesy down in the cistern in his underwear. As he swam around, we lowered the jugs for him to gently float.

Mission accomplished, we pulled him back from the hole, replaced the lid, and made our escape (after Jonesy toweled off and put his clothes back on).

Each day we would have to jump down there and release the carbon dioxide. Genius!

Or stupid.

You decide.

Hey, weren't we drinking that water in the cistern?

Isn't Jonesy's ass in that water?

Details, Details.

I didn't drink the water.

That's always a solid plan to live by.

Drink the beer, steer clear of the water.

Wear a condom.

Wait, I'm getting off topic.

Look close. Jonesy treading water down in the cistern hanging 10! Ha!

Chapter 34
Greener Acres

Relatively speaking, we were going from Compton to the hills of Hollywood. Goodbye, expandable freezing shit hole! Helloooo, marble floored heaven!

We had gotten the word one day that our house was ready to occupy. The air conditioners were installed, the water was flowing, and the toilets flushed. We took what few possessions we had, threw them into the bus, and never looked back.

Goodbye expandable meat locker! Willy and Cowboy.

I was first through the door, and immediately went to the last room down the hall, furthest from the front door, and right next to the bathroom. This seemed like the best room to me, since no one had any reason to be near my door unless they were coming to my room. Plus, being next to the bathroom is always a bonus.

I threw my bag in the corner, and Jonesy threw his crap on the other side of the room. We were going to bunk two per room, kind of.

As predicted, Sgt. Asswipe Fox grabbed the only room with its own private bathroom, and then, just like in the White Palace, he announced he wasn't taking a roommate.

Therefore, three guys would end up sharing one of the rooms.

They say you can't change the spots on a dick, and Fox proved it again.

Luckily, the very first room inside the front door was extra large, so three people easily fit, but it was still a dick move.

Cowboy and Dunc took the room closest to mine, just on the other side of the bathroom. The other five guys split the two rooms at the front of the house.

When we first moved in, there was zero furniture. We had to use our military cots for sleeping and the living room was bare. We were told furniture would be coming eventually. We looked around and saw the potential of our house.

Who would believe we'd be ramping up for a war from the comfort of a marble-floored house?

Incredibly surreal.

Life for the firemen was about to change again and I could never have imagined what was to come next.

One of the bedrooms, pre furniture.

Chapter 35
Jesus Didn't make Iced Tea

Jesus had a lot of choices to make during his life.

Sit in the middle of the big table, or to one of the sides.

Twelve disciples or eleven?

Sandals or boots?

But when the party ran out of wine, he didn't decide that everyone had had enough. He had a decision to make and he made the right one.

How do we *know* it was the right one? Because his *mom* told him to make more wine, and a good son always does what his mom asks.

What does this have to do with a bunch of thirsty firemen in the desert?

We all loved our mothers.

Geez. Pay attention.

Soon, it became abundantly clear what our world now revolved around.

Wine.

With wine, all other things just came easy.

As soon as we were settled into our new abode, we made sure our wine was happy but quickly came to a conclusion. As soon as our wine was ready to drink, we would easily run through it faster than the next batch would be done. It took us about three weeks from start-to-finish making a batch of Desert Malmac, and by anyone's best guess, we would probably be able to empty every bottle within two or three days, four if we really tried.

Rut Row.

What to do? What to do?

We immediately pulled our money and drove to the grocery store in Riyadh. It was time to get batch number two started. No time to waste.

We bought the ingredients the same way we did the first time. Divide and conquer.

We drove back to the new house and immediately got to work. If we really ramped this up, we might never run out of wine. The only problem to overcome was where to hide all of these wine bottles after the first batch was ready. It's funny how you come up with crazy solutions to wacky problems when you take the time and have the resources.

Jonesy, me and Cowboy. Getting a new batch going.

We were still using the cistern, but we also used our old box to allow the next four jugs of wine to ferment. Making the wine wasn't the problem now, but hiding so much wine was going to be a challenge.

Cowboy and I were coming up with solutions to the problem without each other knowing.

Back in ninth grade, all boys were required to take shop. We were taught how to put a new plug on a power cord, what sandpaper was, and how to use every type of power tool. I was never great at making any of the silly projects that the teacher required us to make but it did give me a basic understanding of how all of the stuff worked. Who knew that this information would ever be useful later? My point is: Stay in school kids. One day you might need a way to hide your wine.

On my off days, I went to the woodshop and began building a bookshelf. I thought it would look like a normal piece of furniture for a bedroom. I could store all of my crap in and on it. But the real reason for building it was for hiding wine. I figured I could make a false back and store several bottles of wine behind it (twenty bottles, to be exact). If it worked, I'd show the other guys how to make one and we could all have handy ways to hide the wine and store our personal items with an attractive bookcase.

Back of secret bookshelf. The front looked "normal"

Cowboy was making something much better. Any house with a flat roof and a tall wall around it to hide the occupant's shenanigans certainly needs ways to entertain not only themselves but guests as well. The only solution was to build a big-ass barbeque.

BIG. ASS. BBQ.

One day I wander up to the roof and there Cowboy is, putting the finishing touches on this gigantic grilling edifice. Wow. Here we were, in some crazy backward, sand-infested country, and Cowboy has installed a BBQ on a roof.

It was so out-of-place looking, you had to laugh.

I was in awe of how handy Cowboy was. This guy had skills. They had taken a 55-gallon drum, cut it for an opening, attached hinges, and then placed it in this huge cabinet. Amazing. He showed me how he attached two large doors on the front to store all of his BBQ making items.

Charcoal, lighter fluid, yadda, yadda, yadda.

Dunc helping Cowboy paint the new BBQ

Having just finished my bookshelf, I had one suggestion for his new handiwork. I suggested putting in a false bottom so we could store about fifty or more wine bottles on their sides. Bam! Cowboy added a few more pieces of wood lickety-split, and the next thing you knew, we were in business. We could now make and store huge quantities of our precious liquid.

We used every single place available to hide our wine, so to not show you the next picture would be a crime. If there was a crazy hiding hole to shove a bottle, we shoved one in there. We took our hiding mandate very seriously, because the wine was the source of so many other things, and to not have this priceless asset was unthinkable.

Jonesy and Cowboy holding up the false bottom to show the wine bottles stored.

Not sure why this little door was there, but we found another use. Jonesy hiding more bottles.

Chapter 36
Foreshadowing Events

A few weeks after everyone was moved into Eskan, the fine people at MWR (Morale, Welfare and Recreation) decided that bored and idle troops were a bad thing. They put their best efforts in and began putting on theme parties on rooftops. They had *tropical* night and *disco* night and several other clever nights. Some of us attended one of the first parties they threw, mainly to see if there were any girls. We hadn't put the finishing touches on our own rooftop, and our wine was still a few days from bottling, so we went to see if they were worth our time.

Sad. It was just sad.

They had music and pretend alcoholic drinks, but it was like they were trying just a little too hard.

By now, I was so miserable about not getting any mail from Martha, I wasn't against seeing if a desert hookup was a possibility. Unfortunately for me, my pickup abilities on even a good day were less-than-decent, and without a snort or five of liquid courage, my hopes of talking up one of the very few women at this party was on par with the Titanic making it to New York. It's ironic that in the Air Force I couldn't find someone to be my wingman in my attempts to find female companionship.

I stayed at the pathetic party just long enough to estimate my odds of meeting someone, or having five minutes of fun, then left. Dunc and Cowboy, however, were apparently playing on a higher level and made some new friends, the pretty kind. These guys had skills 'ole Jim neither understood nor mastered. But there was hope in my future.

Since we had a new city, we needed a fire department. One of the houses at Eskan Village was turned into our third fire department. This was *the* place to work. Why? Because it was so ar away from any type of supervision, it made it a perfect place to hide.

After you made the morning inspection of your firetruck, you had absolutely zero responsibilities except deciding when to eat lunch and dinner. To combat the boredom, we stocked the place with every board game we could get our hands on. We also had a television hooked up to a VCR. People were sending us loads of VCR cassettes so we had plenty to watch. It was also a good place to catch up on sleep.

However, one day, we had visitors. *Girl* visitors.

They came out to visit the firemen on duty, and lucky me, one of the girls turned out to be the girl of my dreams, Mary.

Good 'ole Eskan Fire Department.

I think Dunc's and Cowboy's new friends had decided Mary and Jim would make a good couple, so a little matchmaking was taking place in the background. At the time, I didn't realize what was happening, but since cluelessness is one of my superpowers, this wasn't a big surprise down the road. It wasn't an immediate success story, however. The lightbulb over my head wasn't entirely plugged in yet.

I'm a work in progress.

Chapter 37
Playing by the Rules.....at First

According to the handbook of illegal and undercover activities, there is a *proper* way to make desert wine. First, you let the brew ferment in your five-gallon gas can. When the liquid stops making gas, it is wine, but there is also a lot of sludge inside. So as not to make wine that you can also chew, you must siphon it into another container so you don't have a bunch of gunk in your bottles later.

Cloudy wine will not win any awards in France.

We learned this important information from our British friends.

After we had siphoned the wine, we waited a few more days for it to clear up, and once again siphoned it into bottles.

Well, most of it we siphoned into bottles.

It was siphoned into several cups at the same time.

I can't tell you what the alcohol content was, but I'd put it on the scale of "ass-kicking content."

When you have that many people in a room with smiles on their faces, you must have done something right. Thus, and forthwith, with a snap of a finger, life instantly changed. I'm pretty sure I heard angels singing in the background.

We had a house with a roof. On the roof sat a big-ass barbeque.

There was only one thing left to do: buy as much meat as we could get our hands on and have a big, motherfucking, rock and roll, kick-ass, Party (see that capital "P"?).

No more themes.

No more pretend alcoholic drinks.

It was time to crank this bitch up a notch or ten.

The weekend was fast approaching and we had shit to accomplish.

For our first party, we were only going to invite a select few. No sense in blowing all of our first batch of wine on just one party. The first people on our list were obviously the girls. It seemed Cowboy and Dunc had already taken care of this part. Really, all I had to do was pony up some money for the supplies and wait for the weekend.

Now, I'd be remiss if I didn't mention the rest of the guys we were with. Most of the others were on the opposite shift. However, they were also having trouble dislodging the stick someone had inserted into their asses. They seemed to be happy most of the time just sitting around and playing cards. Their sense of adventure, or maybe their common sense, made them a little wary of participating in our fiendish plans to make alcohol and party hearty. They liked the idea of "drinking" the alcohol, but the making and party part weren't very exciting to them. Even worse, when it came time to ask for a little cash to buy the alcohol making supplies, they downright refused. It was hard to share a glass of wine with a fellow troop who refused to pony up for the grocery bill. It was a source of tension for our entire stay.

Fox on the other hand, was his own special head case. He distanced himself from our vino making activities, for fear of being caught and having a shit storm rain down upon his head. Technically, he was still in charge of our group from Eaker, so if we got in trouble, he got in bigger trouble. He would occasionally warn us to stop our activities, but we would remind him that it was his ass that got this party officially started, so he could just shut the hell up. It was obvious he was just covering his own ass. He just came off as spineless, and lost what little respect anyone had left for him.

Recently, we had noticed helicopters were flying relatively low over Eskan Village. Initially, we were unsure of what they were doing. Being the paranoid band of winemaking outlaws we were, we decided we did not need people in helicopters watching us eating hot dogs and burgers while opening several bottles of our delightful, purple libations.

The answer was simple.

We had access to loads of military stuff, and a few, slightly expensive, radar deflecting, camo nets wouldn't be missed.

Once we *liberated* these nets, we hung them in fashionable yet strategic ways to hide prying eyes from "need to know" parties.

Now we were ready.

We later discovered that the guys in the helicopters were actually taking pictures of girls who were sunbathing naked.

I guess it really wasn't all about us. Go figure.

Roof configured to party! Me, Renate and Cowboy.

Chapter 38
Let the Good Times Roll!

The invitations were sent. All we had to do was wait for the weekend and make sure we had our food supplies ready to roll out.

Out of the thousands of military people over here, we were pretty sure we were the only group of people who had alcohol, or at least to this large of a degree. Sure, some people were probably getting a bottle or two mailed to them now and then, but we suddenly had over fifteen gallons of high octane vino.

Yowza!

Goodbye, sad MWR theme parties.

Hello, BBQ and music and wine!

Cowboy was rocking the BBQ as night began to fall. He looked very at home flipping burgers and hot dogs over an open flame. The term "laid back" would fit perfectly.

Buns, ketchup, baked beans, mustard, relish.

We did this right.

Soon, people started filing in. When they first saw our setup, they had to smile and some even laughed. Apparently, few people were going out of their way to make their houses livable. We were going the extra mile at all times.

But when we handed them their first glass of wine, the first glass that many had had in weeks or months, I think a few people may have teared up a little bit. Just kidding, military people don't cry.

They took that first drink like they didn't believe it was real, but they soon discovered the truth. Maybe it wasn't Napa Valley quality, but it was drinkable, and it quickly put you in the mood to party.

As the sun set over the desert sand, the wine flowed and everyone was happy. This felt good.

The smell of someone cooking over an open flame, music playing, plenty of wine.

The first party wasn't the "blowout" that they eventually became, but it was perfect.

We talked and drank and laughed for hours. No one wanted it to end, but when you knew you had to get up in a few hours to go to work, it couldn't last forever. That was okay. We never told anyone to leave our parties but when the wine bottles stopped appearing, the party would naturally wind down. This was just the first of many memorable nights.

I'm not sure how many bottles we went through that first party, but it nearly wiped us out. The coming out party was a success in countless ways. It quickly established the firemen's house as *the* place to be.

Want to drink and have a great party? Find the firemen.

As time went on, the parties got bigger, more elaborate and more outlandish.

If there was a way to raise the bar, or in some people's opinions, lower the bar, we were there to break the bar.

We brought a fire pit on the roof, because you can't have a good party without a fire pit. But we didn't stop there.

Games, we needed games because just getting ripped off your ass is never enough. First, we introduced "Challenge Twister in your Underwear".

Why?

Don't ask why or you begin to break down the entire social structure we were trying to establish.

We were busy smashing together M*A*S*H and Stripes into a new lifestyle. After that, someone found a croquet set.

How do you sit up a croquet set on a tile roof?

Again, don't ask stupid questions. We made it happen.

Over the course of the next few months, we strung Christmas lights (oops, there's that Christ thing again), played loud music and made wine as fast as we could get the yeast to cooperate. Eventually, things began to get out of hand. We were becoming a

little too well known and I, for one, thought we were getting pretty close to being caught.
We were practically flaunting our wealth and fame.
Things were flying off the roof.

The girls came to join the fun.

Why play in your underwear? Why not!

Inspecting the next play.

We were loud.

You could smell the BBQ cooking and hear the laughter for blocks.

I felt trouble was coming and I thought there was only one thing to do.

Invite the people to the party who might actually have the power to get us in trouble. The more "higher ups" we could pull into this circle, the safer we were.

The first guy was easy, and it turned out to be a great idea for a lifetime. We invited our Assistant Fire Chief into our lifestyle.

It really didn't take much encouragement.

Anyone who is cut off from alcohol and the company of nice women for any amount of time isn't going to put up much of a fight.

Tom was cool, in every way. As a boss, he used common sense and was a great buffer between the troops and crazy Tribuck. But as we spent more "roof time" with Tom, he ended up becoming an awesome friend for life. More would come later.

There are plenty more "roof stories" to tell, and we will get to them eventually, but plenty happened along the many months that we were there, so let's not spoil the fun and tell them all at once. Be sure that the parties became bigger and more outrageous.

We were living on some other planet.

Our "pre-war" time left us with lots of time to get in lots of trouble, and it's amazing that we're not all in Leavenworth.

Chapter 39
China Beach

Through the mirror of my mind
Time after time
I see reflections of you and me
Reflections of
The way life used to be......

Every good war movie has a soundtrack, and ours was no different. Before we left for this adventure, I was (and still am) a huge fan of the show *China Beach*. If you aren't familiar, it's the story of Vietnam told from the point of view of a close group of people working at a medical unit, kind of like *M*A*S*H*. The soundtrack to the show seemed to mirror much of how we felt and what was going on around us. It was one of the few cassette tapes I brought with me, and I played it relentlessly. I never got bored with the songs, and no one else complained, so it got played. A lot.

In fact, I played the poor tape so much, I eventually wore it out. One day, it just stopped working.

I was not happy.

It wasn't like I could pop down to my local music store and buy a new tape.

Yes, they sold cassette tapes in Saudi Arabia, but surprisingly, most of the ones we found were pirated. There was an actual shopping mall in downtown Riyadh, and even their stores seemed to only sell pirated music tapes. They were in weird, plastic cases and someone had apparently made bad copies of the cover art or picture and stuck in on the front of the case. You got what you paid for when you bought one of these. Sometimes they worked, and sometimes you didn't get the music advertised on the case. It was a crazy crap shoot, which also made it funny. Each cassette cost about $2.00, so no matter how bad it was, you weren't out much money. However, there was no *China Beach* soundtrack.

I immediately wrote my roommate Drew a letter. I told him to get off his lazy ass, buy me another cassette, and mail it to me yesterday. I knew how motivated Drew was on a daily basis, so I tried to put the proper words together so he would understand how important this was the troops. Letter mailed. We waited.

To my surprise, in less than two weeks, my envelope arrived with my new *China Beach* cassette. Once again, our lives had a soundtrack to move by. It's hard to explain how listening to these songs in that place was different than listening to them before. Or listening to them if you've never experienced circumstances like we were living. I think that's why no one tired of the soundtrack. It felt like there were others before us who could understand what we were going through and were about to go through. That seemed to mean something to each of us at the time. Rock on, *China Beach*. Rock on.

Chapter 40
Modern Living

When we moved into our new houses, they were bare. We had to bring our cots with us to sleep on and continue to use our sleeping bags. It was like camping in your house. We were told that furniture would eventually show up, just be patient. Buying, transporting and delivering thousands of beds and other furniture was going to take a little time.

So we waited. We had a nice kitchen with a stove, sink, and refrigerator, so it wasn't very hard to wait. We had been sleeping on cots for so long now, missing a bed wasn't a big deal.

We even had a special bathroom. The first time we walked into the bathroom, we were a bit baffled. Why did they have two toilets in each bathroom, and why did only one have a seat? Finally, one of the more worldly roommates spoke up and pronounced this second toilet as a *bidet*.

One of us turned it on and it resembled a gigantic water fountain.

We all giggled like little girls.

Who was going to test this out?

No one volunteered.

I hate to admit this, but in the end (pun intended), some of the guys started washing their clothes in this thing. Personally, I never did give the thing a spin as it was intended. I guess I'm not as worldly as I thought.

After a few weeks, everyone received an actual bed with sheets and a comforter. *Sweeeeeet!* That was all for now. We were assured a dresser and headboard would soon follow. A few days later a couch and entertainment center showed up, and a television to boot. We could now watch a few very select cable stations, but CNN was our favorite.

Why? Because they were devoting an incredible amount of coverage to Desert Shield. We could keep up-to-date on what was happening to us faster than the brass were willing to tell us over here.

We also had a phone installed. It could not only call locally but if you were willing to whip out your credit card, you could place a call anywhere in the world. We did. The only downside was that it was incredibly expensive. Calls home were short.

After a few weeks, we had completely outfitted houses.

Bed with headboards.

Dressers.

Nightstands.

We jazzed it up with our own special bookshelves and rugs bought at the Batha. As far as living standards went, we were living pretty high on the hog. I'm sure the camel riding goat herders were comfortable too, somewhere out there. I could see how this could turn into quite the vacation for some people. Why leave? It beat the crap out of Arkansas. Sorry, Razorbacks.

Jonesy napping. Bed. Headboard. Dresser. Secret bookshelf.

Chapter 41
The Popcorn Incident

Work was fairly normal, but it didn't need to be. We wanted to cut out the stupid duties we didn't need to be doing in Saudi Arabia but Tribuck was having none of that. As long as bombs weren't actively falling from the sky, or terrorists weren't sniping at us, there was no reason to not be doing everything just like back home. He asked us to start washing the fire trucks on a regular basis. We just about shit.

Wash the fire trucks?

These fucking fire trucks?

These brown ones, sitting on the edge of a desert?

What "dirt" exactly did he think was getting on these fucking things?

There was no dirt!

We hadn't seen even a cloud in months, so there were no mud puddles, no dirt patches, no any-fucking-thing to get these trucks "dirty." All he wanted us to do was be busy. Wash things that weren't dirty. Mop things that some other guy already mopped. He was starting to fuck up a good thing here. The saying, "Tribuck is fucking crazy," began to be worthy of a bumper sticker. God (or Allah) help a poor fireman standing around for five minutes without something to do.

This went on for weeks, but that wasn't the straw that broke the camel's back. It was the popcorn situation.

Our friendly people at MWR would loan out equipment for the troops to use for a week or two, then turn back in so the next person or group could use. Early on, the fire department had checked out the popcorn popper. It was one of those small, carnival-sized poppers that had glass around it. Put some corn in the little pan, turn it on, and soon, *popcorn!* It was a nice little treat to have in this crap hole.

After we turned it back in, Tribuck checked it back out.
For himself.
He kept it in his office, which he kept locked.

The poor, lonely, mistreated, sad firemen had no access to the delicious, fluffy popcorn. Weeks went by. Tribuck decided that instead of turning in the popcorn popper, he would just keep signing it back out. I don't know if he was technically breaking a rule, but he was technically being a dick.

I'm not sure why it set him off at exactly that moment, but our usually soft spoken, easygoing, jovial Cowboy lost his shit. Big time lost it.

We were all sitting around the fire department on the flight line. There must have been a popcorn conversation, if you can imagine a popcorn conversation. All of a sudden, Cowboy says in a loud voice, "That's bullshit!" and starts stomping off towards the fire chief's office.

Tribuck's office. As he's making his way there, Senior Airman Chandler (Cowboy) is yelling how it's not fair that Buck has had the popcorn popper for so long to himself and that he needs to turn it back in so other people can check it out (mainly us).

The rest of us are trailing behind Cowboy. Some are trying to slow him down to get him turned around. Some are coming along to just watch whatever happens next, because some good entertainment is about to take place.

Cowboy is already yelling at Master Sergeant Tribuck before he even gets to his door.

"BUCK!"

Not even Tribuck, or Sergeant Tribuck, but "BUCK!" "BUCK!"

As he gets to the office door, Tribuck is standing in his office, merely feet away from the popper in question, as Cowboy lays into him.

"Goddamnit, Buck! That popcorn popper is for everyone! You've had that thing for weeks and we can't use it because you lock your door! You need to turn it back in so everyone can check it out!"

Holy *shit* you should have seen the look on this old man's face! It was such a mixture of shock, embarrassment, and anger that I've not seen anything like it before or since. Here was this lowly airman, cussing and screaming at this grizzled old master sergeant over a fucking popcorn popper.

It was otherworldly.

Finally, Cowboy stopped yelling, and Buck's mouth was just hanging open. What would happen next? If this were a television show, the commercial break would be inserted, because no one was tuning away from this train wreck. When he picked his jaw off the floor, the first thing he could stammer out was, "You guys can come here and get popcorn whenever you want."

"That's bullshit!" Cowboy shot back.

He really just yelled "bullshit!" Oh, this was CLASSIC!

"You keep this office locked when you're not here!" Cowboy yelled.

"Well, I'll keep it unlocked," Buck shot back, but that wasn't good enough.

"Just turn it back in Buck, other people want popcorn too!"

Buck's face was about as red as a baboon's ass, but before the show could continue, Tom finally got Cowboy by the arm and said in his best Assistant Chief's voice, "Come on, Cowboy." Buck and Cowboy just glared at each other, time seemed to stand still, and the rest of us just watched to see how the showdown would end.

Would Buck send him to the stockades?

Would Cowboy grab the popper and stalk out?

After a few more hour-like seconds, Cowboy let Tom lead him away.

The next day, the popcorn popper was returned to MWR.

Master Sergeant Tribuck never mentioned the incident.

Cowboy became a legend.

I think people still sit around campfires in the old west and sing songs about that day.

I know I do.

The LEGEND OF COWBOY and THE POPCORN POPPER ives on.

MWR. Look closely, popcorn popper on far right.

Chapter 42
It's a Love Story, Really

As the roof parties and occasional British Compound visits progressed, our mutual friends schemed like Cupid's accomplices. The first few times Mary and I met, I was a bit slow on the uptake, as I am somewhat known to be. However, once I got close enough to look into those blue eyes, I saw something I hadn't experienced before or since.

I just wanted to keep looking and never stop.

What the hell was wrong with me?

I later found out.

I fell in love.

Yup, this went from a wine making war story to a love story, just like that. BAM! But there were complications. I was engaged, and I eventually discovered she was engaged too. Lucky for both of us, our "others" were asses that didn't deserve either one of us. Lucky, right?

For several weeks in the fall of 1990, in the desert sands of a foreign land, while waiting for a war to start, two people found each other.

To be fair, there were several hook-ups happening, and it was anyone's guess just how long they would last, but according to Sgt. Glass Half Empty Pennington, half of us were bound to die, so why die alone?

It's interesting how the circumstances of being here seemed to intensify everything around us. Funny things were funnier. The wine was stronger. The friendships we made were etched in stone a bit deeper. I think everyone experienced this, and I was no different.

One afternoon, we were invited to a wave pool. MWR had set up a special trip for us to visit a local pool. Normally, the Saudi people would gather here as families and experience the waves and cool water of this man-made ocean in the desert. However, for one day, they closed the park to let just the military people use it. Allah forbid that we see any of the local women without their costumes.

I asked Mary to go and we loaded into a tour bus and headed to the beach. It was just like the wave pools in the USA, one big wave pool with lots of umbrella tables nearby. Mary and I spent a lot of time in the pool together until our friend, Mike, almost killed himself. He flew down one of the water slides and whacked his head hard enough that he probably ended up with a concussion, putting the kibosh on the rest of Mike's day. As friends do, we made sure he stayed alive until we boarded the bus back to reality.

By late October, it looked like the both of us had decided whatever was going on, we didn't want it to end. We were inseparable. If we were in the same room, or on the same roof, there wasn't a space between us, and I was plenty fine with that.

But nothing works out perfectly.

There was a monkey nearby and he grabbed the nearest wrench and threw it directly at us.

She had to leave.

Mary was in the Air Force Reserves and their orders only kept them in Saudi Arabia for a month. That month was almost over.

Shit on a stick. Now what?

We'd have to play this by ear, but we knew one thing: we didn't want this to end. We made plans.

Roof time with Mary

Chapter 43
Private Sausages

Not all of our parties were massive blowouts. During the week, we often had a kind of couples' party in Cowboy's and Dunc's room. It wasn't always just for couples, since sometimes one of us didn't have their person with them, but most of the time it was no larger than six of us.

We would grab a few bottles of wine, a summer sausage, some cheese and mustard. We'd light a few candles, turn off the lights, fire up the China Beach soundtrack, close the door and just sit around for hours and talk. We laughed a lot and told stories. These were some of the best times we had.

Poor Jonesy was in sad shape. It seemed like the harder he tried to find a girl, the more they avoided him. Maybe it was that desperate look on his face. He wanted so badly to be with the couples' group, it was killing him. Now and then we'd let Jonesy come to the little party in Cow's room. I think he felt good knowing he was included and was around some girls, but deep down, he just seemed sad. I felt bad for him, but he usually ended up saying something inappropriate, and my sadness for him just melted away. He was his own worst enemy.

Our little subgroup always made sure to stash a few bottles of wine and a few sausages away somewhere, just for these little get-togethers. All was fine, and for a brief blip on the radar screen, I didn't want to be anywhere else, doing anything else, with anybody else. Hang out with friends, workout at the makeshift gym, work every other day, party on the roof, and spend time with Mary.

Then she left.

Her time had come to leave, and she boarded the plane and left the desert sands behind. And me.

Sadness followed, and our little summer sausage parties were never the same. There was now a hole in my life.

Chapter 44
YE FUCKING HA!

Life looked down on Jonesy and me one day, saw we were both kind of low, and decided that it was going to give us a reason to smile again, even if it was only for a brief while. We were walking across Eskan Village and saw a helicopter flying low, coming in for a landing nearby. Having nothing better to do, we made our way to the landing zone. Helicopters are cool, and the people who fly around in them are cool, and standing next to one is cool. Wanting some of the coolness to rub off on us, we asked the pilot if we could take a few pictures of their awesome Black Hawk helicopter. They, being the cool people they were, said, "Sure."

With the shitty little camera always kept nearby, I started taking pictures of Jonesy and me standing next to the awesome machine.

Playing helicopter Maverick

Because we were just hanging out at Eskan, we were both wearing T-shirts and shorts. No big deal. I climbed into the cockpit and Jonesy snapped my pic. I took one of him. Before the pilots walked off to grab some lunch, they asked us a question that I'll never forget.

"Wanna go for a ride?"

What??

Do I want to ride in your magical, fucking awesome *Black Hawk helicopter*?? Giggle, giggle, giggle.

But what we really said, with the biggest grin a face can make was, "Hell yeah!"

He said, "You have to be in uniform, and have permission from your supervisor. Also, this is a one way trip, so you'll have to find a ride home from the next base we're going to."

Yes! Yes! And they better say yes!

They told us to meet them back at the chopper (that's what we cool military folks refer to our birds as) in a hour. We ran.

We had to be careful which supervisor to ask.

Tribuck? Hells no! That dick would just say no because he's a dick.

Fox? Hmmmmm. He'd probably say no because it was easy and he wasn't invited.

Tom? Tom was a fun-loving, adventurous dude who would never deny a few of his troops the ride of a lifetime!

Right?

So we found Tom and told him our story.

Tick Tock. He didn't even hesitate.

"Sure. Just be back for shift tomorrow," he said.

Fuck yeah!

We sprinted to our room and quickly changed clothes.

We met the pilots back at the helicopter. Both rear side doors were open and they asked if we had permission. We both said, "Yeah," and that was it.

They just took our word for it, which was good, because that's all the hell we had. We hadn't even thought about having someone write something on a piece of paper to sign. What would we even had written, and how would they know who signed it? It wasn't like there was some official form for letting some Air Force firemen take a joy ride in a helicopter. Was there?

Who cares, because they just said, "Okay, get in and put your seatbelts on." We climbed in and my heart was actually beating like I was about to have my first kiss.

This was fucking awesome! Oh, man!

What's hilarious was, we didn't know where this next base they were flying to actually was, or how far away it was, or how we were going to find a ride back to Eskan. All we knew was that we were going to be flying in a Black Hawk fucking helicopter.

As the rotors began to fire up, they told us to put on our headsets so we could hear and talk to each other. This was good, because these guys didn't even close the side doors, and the blades outside were loud. Soon, we felt the skids leave the ground, and we were in the air. As we rose into the sky, watching Eskan get smaller beneath us, Jonesy and I looked at each other, and we were both smiling ear to ear.

Holy shit. We were flying in a motherfucking Black Hawk helicopter!

Best war ever!

Soon, it became apparent that these pilots were having a good time too. They were going to test how big the balls were on the two Air Force guys. They stayed fairly low to the ground, only about two hundred feet in the air, and started pushing this machine for all it was worth. They would bank it so hard to the left, and then to the right, that the entire helicopter was on its side. If we weren't strapped in tight, we would both have fallen right out the side door. Instead of screaming like little girls, we were both going "Wooooooooo Hoooooooooooooo!" like we were on the best roller coaster ever.

What these guys didn't know about their firemen in the back seat was that Jonesy and I had taken up skydiving several months ago. Soon after I had arrived at Eaker AFB, a group of guys said they were going skydiving the next weekend. I had never really entertained the idea, because I didn't realize that just anyone could go do that. So off we went one Saturday.

Rocking the mustache and the Ray Bans!

Jonesy looking cool. Not hard in a helicopter!

We did the little course and started with little "hop and pops" from a Cessna 182. Some of the guys never came back, but from that day onward, I was hooked. I went every other weekend, so by the time this helicopter was flying sideways over the desert sands, I had just under one hundred jumps under my belt, and Jonesy had several as well. We had already done just about one of the scariest things a human can do: voluntarily leave an airplane in flight, so this helicopter ride was just pure adrenaline fun for us. We "whooped" and "whooped" just about all the way to the next base. It was one of those moments in your life you never forget.

Sooner than we liked, we landed. We unbuckled, took off our headsets, did a little high five in slow motion for the movie cameras, and got out of the helicopter as the rotors slowed to a stop. We said "thank you" several times, shook their hands, and made our way to the nearest building, hoping to find a ride home. We lucked out. There were daily military trips between our bases, and we were welcome to hitch a ride. Some days you just get lucky.

What had taken a half hour to fly, was now going to take us two or three hours to drive back. Who cared? It was an adventure I have never forgotten.

Also, Army helicopter pilots are fucking awesome!

Thanks, dudes, wherever you are.

Chapter 45
Murray, not Bill

Another important figure that made this all work was Murray. He came with Buck and was the second in Command. Murray was the buffer between Buck and the rest of the troops and he was good at it. His sense of humor was the perfect fit for the job. If a problem was getting out of control, Murray knew how to bring the tension back down on all sides. This was a good man to have around in a pre-war situation with a bunch of bored firemen.

Murray was also the *master of the scam*. As soon as he arrived, he apparently started making contacts and got the lay of the land extremely quickly. He kept a low profile most of the time, but if you needed something, Murray could make it magically appear or happen.

That is a useful gift in the military. For instance, after we received our televisions at our houses, we speculated how nice it would be to have a VCR to watch all of our tapes that people were sending us. We had a VCR at the fire department, but one at the house would be nice.

"Come with me," Murray said.

We jumped in his truck and drove to a gated area inside ELF1. Murray produced a key from his pocket, unlocked the gate, and inside we went. Murray had a sly smile on his face. Inside the gate was a small mountain of wooden crates. These were things that people had mailed the service people here. He led us to a section that had loads of VCRs.

"Help yourselves," he said.

We all smiled at each other and went to work sorting through the VCRs until we found ones that we liked. There were so many, we could afford to be that picky. We also gathered a few more items that seemed to need a home and back to the truck we went.

This wasn't called stealing; we called it "liberating."

Hey, if we can liberate a country, we can "liberate" a VCR. Right?

Murray made stuff like this happen all of the time, so it took us about five seconds to make sure he was invited to the rooftop parties. He ended up being an even harder partier than we were, which was a hard thing to top.

A wicked sense of humor and quick with a joke, he was a great guy to have around. Once the shit began to hit the fan months later, he and Tom were great guys to have watching our backs. As hard as we tried to get in trouble, they tried harder to keep us out of the shit storm. We were full-time jobs, but they did it with style and made it all seem easy. We were anything but easy.

Chapter 46
Becoming a Local

It takes a certain amount of balls, guts, sense of humor, and *I don't give a fuck* attitude to do what Cowboy and Dunc did for their next trick. I'm pretty sure that no other American in the entire military did what happened next. I'm not sure what our General from earlier in the story would think if he got wind of this latest escapade. If it weren't for the pictures, it might be hard to picture or believe. Prepare yourself.

While we were trying to get lost at the Batha, we noticed several shops sold large bongs. At least that's what we called them.

They stood about three feet high and had one or more pipe pieces that came off the bottom for people to smoke at the same time. There was a metal bowl at the top for the hot coals and *stuff* to smoke. It looked very mysterious, and from my knowledge of what they were used for in America, illegal.

But not here.

Here, they were called *hookahs* and not only were they legal, but an entire part of the Saudi culture was built around them.

While alcohol was strictly forbidden, there were hookah bars all over the place. These were places where only men could visit. Once inside, you sat on the floor, inside little square walled areas, lined with pillows and rugs. The walls around each area were about two feet high, so you could see all the other people in their little areas. As Americans, we were not welcomed. No one told us not to go, but we weren't sure of the protocols, so we stayed clear.

Men only?

Why would we go anyhow?

We all became good friends with Saud and Sadik but Cowboy and Dunc became the best of friends with them. They scored us an invitation to Saud's house for dinner one evening. This was going to be an interesting experience.

It was Jefferys' birthday, and this was going to be a little treat for him as well, so he was asked to come along. Cowboy, Dunc, Jonesy, Jefferys and I were ushered into Saud's house. It was a larger, somewhat modern house, at least by Saudi standards. Saud's family appeared to be wealthy. Maybe all Saudis were this wealthy.

Once upstairs, we were taken to a dining room, but there was no table, just a rug and pillows on the floor. We were told to sit and be comfortable.

His mother and, I can only guess, his sisters, brought us food as we sat in a circle on the floor. I can't tell you who was who, because they were wearing the black abayas. Saudi people eat with their hands, and since I didn't see a fork or spoon in my general vicinity, I just dug right in with everyone else.

There is clearly not a double-dip rule in this culture, so you either got over that quickly, or you didn't eat.

Strong, hot, sweet tea was served to drink, from little cups. It was quite the experience. But the party had barely started.

Some time ago, Saud and Cowboy had this bet that we would all go out on the town together. Saud would dress like an American, and Cowboy and Dunc would dress like Saudis. After a few weeks of going back and forth and laughing about what a fun time this would be, tonight was the night. After dinner, Saud took us to his bedroom, and presented Cow and Dunc with their evening wear. It was full on Saudi robes, headdress, and all. They even threw in some prayer beads to give it the full-on authentic look. We couldn't stop laughing as these guys were getting dressed. It was hilarious!

Once dressed, the moment of reckoning came. Were they brave enough to actually walk out the door and go to a hookah bar?

They were.

However, Saud and Sadik dressed in their normal clothes. They didn't think they would be allowed into the bar wearing American clothes.

Also, they couldn't fit into Cowboy's jeans.

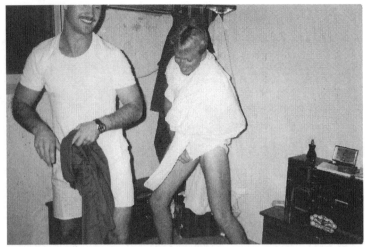
Turning Saudi

The finished product. Cowboy, Sadik, Saud, Dunc. They rocked it!

Outside we all went, laughing our asses off. We got into Saud's car and drove to the bar. As we walked to the front door, it resembled a movie set. We could have just walked out of a time machine and landed in this same place a thousand or more years ago.

Welcome to a thousand years ago. Lights were only modern touch.

Once inside, we were shown to our sitting area. Dunc and Cowboy were swinging their prayer beads in circles. Dunc, never one to be shy, was trying to talk to anyone within earshot. He was throwing out every Arabic word Saud and taught him.

He was going to play this up to the hilt.

The older men in the bar just looked on in amazement or disgust. It was hard to tell the difference.

But no one told us to leave, so we just went with it.

Our waiter came to take our order but it wasn't for food. He asked us what did we want to put in the hookah bowl to smoke. We let Saud make this decision for us, since we had no idea what was going on. In the end, they brought us two different hookahs to smoke from.

Not being a smoker even a little bit, this was going to be interesting, if not embarrassing.

Next came the tea. Again, small cups with extremely sweet, hot tea was passed around.

How did these people not have diabetes and tooth decay was amazing.

As we sipped our tea, the hookah bowels were brought with whatever it was we were supposed to smoke. It was such a bizarre experience.

Seeing all of the other men in their areas, holding hands and looking way too cozy was a bit much for this twenty-six-year-old at the time. Back home, this would be a gay bar.
Maybe it was here too, and Saud was having the laugh of a lifetime at our expense. Either way, we had a blast. A glass or three of wine would have helped quite a bit.

Server bringing bowls.

Dunc swings his beads, Saud on left, Jefferys looking on in amazement.

Group photo. Me, Cow, Sadik, Saud, Dunc and Jefferys.

Chapter 47
Lucky, Lucky Fire Dogs

While we were lucky to have the company of pretty girls, these particular girls were on flight crews. They were medical technicians on large aircraft that transported sick and wounded military people from the Middle East to Germany, the closest large military medical facilities. While in Germany, the crews would have a few hours, or even days, layover. When we discovered this little fact, we started making requests.

Might you wonderful girls pick up a few (as many as you can) bottles of alcohol and bring it back to your firemen?

Yes, we were asking them to break laws and take chances, but desperate times, desperate measures, yadda, yadda, yadda.

Every now and then, as our wonderful, new accomplices in crime made trips to and from the land of schnitzel and sauerkraut, we were supplemented with bottles of rum, whiskey and the like. They were like "rum runners" from the past. Very romantic and sexy, right?

Those were the weeks that the parties took on an extra special tone.

Yes, yes, to those who have turned the pages of my photo album for Desert Shield/Storm, it does look more like a crazy drinking vacation than some sad war story.

Maybe we just did war better than most people.

It takes imagination to turn lemons into lemonade.

We turned a war into a commercial for visiting Saudi Arabia.

I hope the statute of limitations has run out by now.

Chapter 48
Out of the Blue

While Mary was home, I wrote Martha a letter telling her that our engagement was over and we were done. I listed all of my reasons, and told her goodbye and have a nice life. I was beyond my limit of her silly antics, and this seemed like the perfect opportunity to finish this.

I was a zillion miles away, so she didn't have the chance to be crazy to my face. Mary seemed more than interested in going forward with our relationship, which was perfect. She also didn't seem secretly crazy, and that was another huge plus. The timing was right.

One day, out of the blue, the phone rang at our house.

It was Martha.

After zero letters, and acting like a stubborn child the few times I tried to call her, here she was calling me. I would have been less shocked if I saw the Loch Ness Monster having afternoon tea with Bigfoot.

I figured the letter must have reached its destination. It had been almost two weeks. She must be calling to try to patch things up.

"Hello," I said, trying to keep my voice steady and not give away the anger I was feeling.

Did she think she was going to fix this now?

Too much had happened. I was going to stick to my guns here.

"Hey, how's it going?" she asked.

She actually sounded kind of happy, like it was just a normal phone conversation. Did she not get the letter yet? Was I gonna have to do this breakup thing here and now on the phone?

Ugh.

My palms started to sweat. This wasn't going to be a good conversation. Trying to cut this off immediately, I asked, "I wrote you a long letter, did you get it?" Silence.

I knew she must have the letter.

"Martha, I explained everything in the letter. You haven't written to me and you didn't talk to me when I tried to call you. That's not the way you treat someone you're supposed to love. We're over."

Silence.

But this time I didn't care how long she stayed silent.

These phone calls to Saudi costs several dollars for every minute, and this was on her dime, not mine.

No more me trying to squeeze in an entire conversation in five minutes.

Her dad was going to have a shit fit when he saw this bill.

Whatever. Not my problem.

So I just said nothing.

And she said nothing.

I was going to just let this keep going until she spoke up or hung up.

Finally, I could tell she was sniffing and maybe crying.

Hold strong, Jim! Don't give in to that crying shit!

"I'll start writing to you," she finally whispered between sobs.

"No," I said, "it's too late for that. I needed you two months ago. I can't be with someone who would treat me like that. It's over, goodbye."

I hung up.

She called back.

I told one of the guys to tell her I wasn't there.

That was the last time I spoke with her until I eventually got back to the United States. She tried to call a few more times, but eventually gave up. That chapter of my life was almost over. Thank goodness! Time to move forward.

Chapter 49
STUFFing

Thanksgiving was approaching. It's weird celebrating holidays pertaining to the United States while being out of the country. A couple of years before this little trip, I was in Austria for vacation on the Fourth of July. I held the door open as I exited a train station as another guy was also exiting. He said, "thank you," in a very "American" sounding accent. I said, "Happy Fourth of July," to which he dryly said, "I'm Canadian."

I never made that mistake again.

You never know how people are going to respond to your American holiday when you are beyond its borders.

One day while we were sitting on the roof, the topic of the turkey was brought up. Maybe it was the wine talking, but suddenly, everyone wanted to make sure we celebrated Thanksgiving as patriotically as possible. Several people made mention that they had some favorite dish from home that they were sure they could recreate over here. It's nice that some people have those skills.

Give me a hot dog, and I'll gladly grill it to perfection.

Give me a turkey, and I'll give it right back.

So it was on. We checked the calendar and made sure we were all off that day. Yup.

Not that it mattered, we could celebrate Thanksgiving any day we wanted.

Thanksgiving morning rolled around, and everyone met at our house to begin cooking. It was incredible. Suddenly, our house began to smell like a house back home that was gearing up for a big Thanksgiving meal. I wasn't sure how it was all going to taste, but the smell alone was enough to put a smile on everyone's faces.

This was something we all needed. I was amazed that a bunch of twenty-somethings could pull this off. The women did most of the heavy lifting, but some of the guys had skills, too, and did their part.

The only snafu came when one of us left the oven door slightly open for a few minutes so we could make sure the stuff inside didn't burn. Unfortunately, we didn't realize the burner knobs were plastic, and were melting.

Melted knobs don't smell so good.

The rest of the day went off perfectly. We sat around eating about the same thing people back home were eating. Paired with some delicious, day old, red ambrosia, it was a great day for the books.

I missed being home with my mom and step-dad, just as I'm sure we all missed someone back home, but being away in crazy circumstances like this made the entire event more powerful. We take these little holidays for granted back home. We see it as something we will always have and the chaos and headaches and football and traffic will always be there for us to enjoy.

But over here, so far away, nothing seemed for sure. Every holiday seemed like a gift and being here with these people was special stuff. I tried to soak it up as it was happening, not wanting to forget the moment. I couldn't wait to get home again, but I wouldn't want to trade this Thanksgiving for anything.

Chapter 50
The Power of Love

The power of love is a curious thing
Make a one man weep, make another man sing
Change a heart to a little white dove
More than a feeling, that's the power of love
-Huey Lewis

Honestly, I'm not much of a "love story" kind of guy. When one comes on television, I change the channel pretty quickly. But that's what you've got here, like it or not. The three-ish weeks Mary and I spent together were powerful. We shoved what felt like a year's worth of living in just those few days together. When she left, I certainly felt lost, like a part of me was missing. Apparently, she did too.

As soon as she arrived home to New Jersey, she made a beeline to her Reserve Staff and requested to be sent immediately back to Saudi Arabia. Wow!

I must have done something right.

As I was flying around in helicopters and watching Cow and Dunc become temporary Saudi citizens, Mary was working on getting back to me. It almost worked.

About six weeks after she left, she contacted me to let me know she had orders back to Saudi Arabia.

Yes!

But not to Riyadh.

Fuck!

She was being sent to Dhahran. Where the hell was Dhahran?

I was sure it was north of Riyadh, maybe closer to Kuwait, but unless someone put a map in front of me, I really didn't know. It wasn't like I could pop on Google Maps and figure it out. We were a million years from that shit happening. Hmmm. At least she would be in the same country, right? (Note to self: Buy more real maps).

I soon discovered, Saudi Arabia is a big, fucking sandbox of a country.

A few weeks later we were able to call each other on "tack" phones. It didn't happen often, simply because no one could know when one of us would be near a phone. I worked every other day at the fire department, so I was usually the easier person to track down. That worked for a while, but "ain't nothing like the real thing baby".

Having a lot of time on my hands, I hatched a plan.

The war was approaching and we knew that in the next few weeks, things were going to change. My time was limited for the scheme I had plotted.

This would go one of two ways: really, really good or crazy bad.

I had to make sure the right people knew what I was going to do and the wrong people never knew what I was about to do. Secrecy was the key. Loose lips sinks blimps, or something like that.

Tom was very sympathetic to my circumstances. He was probably a poet at heart, but no one would admit that kind of shit in the desert. I went to Tom and casually said, "Hey, Tom. Are we allowed to rent cars in Riyadh?"

"I guess so," he said, eying me suspiciously.

"What if someone were to rent a car and drive to Dhahran and be back the same day, do you think anyone would care?" I asked with a goofy grin. Better to keep questions in the "hypothetical" realm.

Tom thought for a second and replied, with a smile on his face and twinkle in his eye, "I wouldn't want to know about it, and as long as they were back for shift the next day, I don't think there would be a problem."

Did I mention Tom was awesome?

The next day, I put the wheels into motion. Literally.

I dressed in my normal off-duty clothes, which were some shorts, running shoes, and tank top. I threw a uniform into a bag and had Jonesy drive me to the car rental shop in Riyadh. I told him to pick me up at 9pm tonight. We had to be inside the gate by 11pm, giving me plenty of leeway. Inside the rental shop, I picked up some small, little five-speed, gave the man wearing the headdress some cash, and with a big-ass map in hand, Oakley sunglasses on, and a lot of hope, headed into the unknown.

Thank goodness for how simple the route was from Riyadh to Dhahran. It was one road.

It was one road for 260 miles.

This was going to take over four hours to drive. One way.

I had no idea at the time.

I saw Dhahran on a map and the road to take me there. Trying to measure the distance was impossible, mostly because everything was in kilometers. I just drove. If you've never driven through Kansas, count yourself lucky, but if you have, picture Kansas, except instead of green, flat land for as far as the eye can see, it's sand.

Sand forever.

From as far as you can see in front of you, behind you, to your left and right. Sand.

One road through the middle of an empty wasteland.

Every now and then, just to prove you were still on planet Earth, you would see an oil refinery shooting fire into the sky, or some single-humpers just standing there, like a mirage.

Not only was I taking a chance on this entire drive, I had no idea exactly where the base was, if I could get onto the base, if Mary was on the base and if she was, if I could find her. You've got to have faith in something I guess and I had faith that this would work.

Somehow.

So on I drove, blaring my China Beach tape, and trying not to think of all of the ways this could go wrong.

Chapter 51
Welcome to Dhahran (Military City?)

After several hours of driving, I could see something in front of me that wasn't desert. Finally. I was at the city gates to Dhahran. Literally. To proclaim its boundaries, there were two huge pillars on either side of the road and a large, elaborate sign held between them and giant swords crisscrossed.

Hmmmm. I think they were trying to make some type of point here.

The wording at the top was in Arabic, of course, but under that, it said, "Welcome to Dhahran Military City".

Military city?

What could that mean?

Are only military people allowed into the city?

I wasn't taking any chances after driving over four hours just to get turned away. I was going to at least look the part, because maybe I didn't look military enough in my shorts and tank top. I pulled over to the side of the road, grabbed my duffle bag and did a quick wardrobe swap. Prest-O, change-O, I now had my BDUs on and looked *military*. Hopefully, this would help.

Imagine driving into a city, trying to find a single person, and having no idea where they were. That's exactly what I was doing.

I figured that she had to be near a flight line somewhere, since she was on an aircrew, so I just looked for airplanes landing and headed that direction.

This was either brilliant, or stupid, but I didn't have much more to go on.

Luckily, the road I was on was pointed pretty much towards what looked like an airport, so I just went with that. The few planes I saw landing and taking off in the distance all seemed like military planes, so that was a good sign. Right?

I came to a gatehouse on the roadway with Saudi military people posted. My palms started to sweat. Yikes.

I was in a stupid little rental car, which didn't exactly scream "military", so I thought I probably looked suspicious.

Maybe the uniform would be good enough.

I drove up slowly and stopped. I tried to play it cool like I'd done this a hundred times and expected to just drive on through. I put a bored look on my face, not the *scared shitless* one I was feeling. He looked at me for a few seconds, and then just waved me through.

Oh, shit! That worked!

Holy Crap Fuck! Now where?

I drove on beyond the view of the gate so the guards couldn't see me stop to ask directions. That wouldn't look very normal, and I was going entirely for *normal*. I found a U.S. military person walking and asked if they knew where the crews were living from the Medical Evac Squadron. I got very lucky, right off the bat. She said all the crews lived in a tent city, and she gave me directions to get me close. Wow, that was easy.

Maybe I wasn't going to jail today after all.

Chapter 52
Double Take

I drove until I could see what looked like a tent city nearby, then grabbed a parking spot in a lot. Time to walk. Everyone I had seen on the base had been in uniform so far, so I didn't feel out of place as I started walking towards the tents. These were "real" tents, not the expandable kind back in Riyadh at ELF1. Good, old-fashioned, military green tents, like on M*A*S*H, but these didn't look as nice.

How is that possible? You'd think shit would have been updated about 1000% by now, but these actually looked twenty years old. I felt bad for the troops up here. We were living in the lap of luxury, and these guys were on a long-term camping trip.

I stopped another person and asked where the Air Vac people's tents were, and again got pointed to another area. I made my way to a tent that had some homemade signs outside that said "69th Air Vac." I started to feel a bit nervous but in a fun, excited way.

Not wanting to walk right in, since this was a female tent, I just yelled, "Anyone home?"

To which I got a, "Come on in," but I could tell it wasn't Mary's voice.

I went inside the tent to find it was sectioned off for different people to have a little privacy. The floor was wooden pallets that they had obviously procured so they didn't have to have a dirt/sand floor. I asked the girl inside if she knew a Mary?

"Yeah, this is her tent, but she's not here right now."

I said, "Crap. I just drove here from Riyadh and I don't have very long, do you know where she is?"

I was hoping the answer wasn't, "She's flying on a mission right now," but I got lucky again.

"I think she's over at the chow hall," she replied.

She pointed me in the right direction, and off I went.

Can you see a pattern here of being lucky when it came to this girl? That's some good fate mojo there!

A few minutes later I found the chow hall. It was also a tent, similar to the one at ELF1 in Riyadh. The door to the tent was a double-door, kind of like a foyer, probably to help keep the sand and flies outside. I walked in and looked to my right, down the row of tables that were mostly empty. It was between lunch and dinner, so not many people would be inside.

No Mary.

I looked to my left and there she was.

Sitting at a table, facing me, with a guy across from her.

She looked up, saw me, then started talking to the guy again. As I watched her, I saw the light bulb go off in her brain. She immediately looked back up at me and smiled like an angel. She stood up as I walked towards her and when we met she just said, "Oh my God!" and we hugged.

Realizing the guy still sitting there, she pulled away and introduced me to the other military guy. We said a brief hello, then she asked, "What are you doing here? How did you get here?" while having this happy, amazed look on her face.

I just said, "I drove here to see you."

We left the tent, holding hands.

I explained what I did and how I was here. I also told her I only had a couple of hours before I had to beat it back to Riyadh so I wasn't missed. We walked to my car and went for a drive. We mostly just drove around the base and talked and held hands. There really wasn't much more that could happen.

Having some *alone* time on this base just wasn't a possibility.

It wasn't set up that way for anyone. I'm sure people were hooking up, but it was something planned and not spur of the moment. This was fine.

This was more than fine.

I couldn't get the smile off my face, and I couldn't stop staring at hers. This was the stuff they wrote songs about and why there's a Hallmark Channel.

We eventually kissed for the last time, said our goodbyes, and I pointed my rental back towards the sand that led to Riyadh.

That would hold me.

That was worth it ten times over.

I drove as fast as the little car would go on the desert highway. The sun was setting, and I needed to be at the car rental shop to meet my ride back to base. All went perfectly, somehow. I blasted into the car rental shop with minutes to spare. I chucked the keys to the man behind the counter, gave him a smile like a thief, and walk outside to meet my ride. Jonesy gave me a weird look when I showed up in my BDU uniform, since when he dropped me off, I had been in shorts. I explained the *military city* thing as we drove back to Eskan.

The caper was complete. Not one hitch. Atlantis!

Chapter 53
Revetments

As much as I'd like to say it was nonstop roof parties and fun with Mary, we actually had some work to do. The President had given Saddam a deadline to get his happy-ass out of Kuwait, or the shit storm was coming. (LINE IN THE SAND, wink wink) As the date drew near, coalition forces (that means all the troops from all the countries helping the USA) began to ramp up.

More trucks. More tanks. More ammo. More people.

We didn't get left out. If the war was coming, we needed to be prepared. How? Revetments.

What in the Sam Hell is a *revetment* you ask? Basically, it's a hole, at least that's what our revetments were.

In order to not let all of our eggs get blown up in one basket, we would separate the eggs. Follow?

In normal terms, that meant, if one bomb hit the fire department, all of the troops and trucks didn't get demolished at the same time. We got the impression they were probably more concerned about the trucks than the troops. In order to accomplish this, it was decided to take each truck, and the truck's crew, to separate locations around the flight line (runways). 'Ole Sadam Dickweed might blow up one truck, but not all of them. Man, the military brains were brilliant.

But we wouldn't just drive the truck out to a spot and park it, then sit around in the truck.

No. No. Nooooooooooooo.

Revetment. Remember?

First, someone told some dudes (maybe chicks, who knows), to take a bulldozer out to special places around the flight line and dig down far enough, long enough, and wide enough, that a fire truck could drive down a sand/dirt ramp and be about halfway under the surrounding ground. After that was done, then contact the firemen, because their asses were about to get busy.

Also, while you have those big 'ole digging machines going, get a backhoe and dig a hole near the first trench. Make it about five feet deep, eight feet long and six feet wide. Like a tiny-ass swimming hole.

Why? Oh, we'll tell them firemen all about that too. Apparently, someone got wind that the firemen weren't exactly putting out the towering inferno every other day, so we had some time to do some manual labor. (Call back to being Civil Engineers)

After the holes were dug, huge kits of poles and radar deflecting camo netting were dropped off at each revetment location. The firemen had to assemble these kits to cover the holes, so Saddam's non-radar using bombs couldn't see our trucks. Yes, we were hiding our equipment from someone who couldn't see it in the first place.

Why? Well, because someone had bought all of this fancy stuff, and then took the time to ship it all the way over to this shit hole, so by God, we were going to use it.

The short answer is, "It's the military."

Off we went. We were back in building shit mode, just like when we arrived. For the next couple of weeks, we stuck poles together, placed poles in and around big holes, and staked it all down so it stayed in place. We got good at doing this. Too good.

Our Saudi friends decided to make their own revetments, (they didn't want to blow up either I guess) but couldn't figure out how to set up the netting part. Guess what happened?

Yup, we were tasked to help them do it, and by help, I mean, we just did it for them.

How about that extra hole, you ask? That was for the troops. The truck had a nice place to hide, but the crews needed a place to hide as well. We hid in a hole.

Sexy, right?

Cow, Me and Dunc, taking netting out of the box.

Dunc's truck's finished Revetment. Ready for the truck to back into.

After they dug the hole, it was our job to fill a ridiculous amount of sandbags, stack them around the outer edge of the hole, and take a 4X4 post and stick it in the middle of the hole to hold up our roof. What roof? The pieces of plywood they provided us. We stacked more sandbags on top of the plywood, and for added measure, we put our cool, camo, radar-deflecting netting over the entire thing. We left an entrance hole to crawl into, and some extra sandbags inside so we could plug it up after we were inside, to keep all of the nasty chemicals away. Eventually, we had several revetments placed around the flight line for every vehicle and crew.

Finished hiding hole for Rescue Crew. Next to "MAIL DISTRIBUTION" area.

Remember our sweet setup at Eskan Village with the delightful fire department that was off the radar? Remember how we had nothing to do all day but sleep off the hangover from the previous night's party?

That came to a crashing end.

Here was another ingenious Tribuck idea. In order to protect the fire department and firetruck, we had to pile sandbags around it.

Thousands of sandbags.

Guess who had to fill those sandbags?

Cowboy and I inside the hiding hole.

One day a dump truck comes by and unloads a shit ton of sand at our front door, as well as a zillion burlap bags and miles of twine. Shit.

Jonesy and I were on duty for a few shifts at this location and we were told to start filling sandbags. For the next several shifts, eight hours a day, we filled sandbags, tied them off and stacked them up.

Hundreds? Thousands? Billions? I have no idea. Probably closer to a billion.

Because we knew this was useless and total bullshit, it made it even worse.

If a missile hit this one house, out of the thousands here, these fucking sandbags weren't going to make an inch of difference. One thing it did do was about break our backs and destroy our hands. We tried doing the job with the big leather gloves, but we couldn't tie the twine around the tops with gloves on. After several hours of this, the sand had rubbed our hands raw. We started coming up with all kinds of crazy ways to make this easier or faster, but it still sucked.

To this day, when I see a sandbag, it gets me in a pissy mood.

Chapter 54
Tribuck

One day, in December, Tribuck came to our morning shift change. He had significantly less hair than the last time I saw him a few days ago.

Significantly less, as in, he was now practically bald, he had no eyebrows and the hair on his arms was now patchy.

For all of the blustery piss and vinegar that he usually projected, he looked rather sheepish.

What the hell was going on? After roll call, everyone went their separate ways. I was just coming on shift, so a few of us walked up to Murray, because he had an abnormal shit-eating grin on his face like he was about to explode.

As soon as Buck beat a hasty retreat back to the safety of his popcornless office, Murray spilled the beans. It seems that 'ole Buck was trying to relive his Vietnam days of glory, and had built himself his very own moonshine still at his house. Nothing like a man's private stash of moonshine. This guy wanted his own alcohol *and* popcorn. Cowboy took care of the popcorn and now it seemed like fate took care of the rest.

Yesterday, Bucky walked into the room with his still. The still then promptly exploded.

It exploded *big.*

We're talking glass windows gone, damage to cement wall, and fire.

Buck was on fire.

Now, because Buck didn't die this was some funny-ass shit. Hell, it would have probably still been funny if he did die. The picture on his face when that still blew up and him running around trying to put himself out was more than most of us could take. We were laughing our asses off! It had burned off most of his hair, eyebrows and arm hair. He eventually just shaved his head to even it all out.

I have no idea if that had anything to do with what happened next, but a few days later, Buck was on his way back home. We were told he was retiring but since no one had gone home for any reason so far, we thought that was probably just a good bullshit story to tell the troops. I guess even a Master Sergeant wasn't immune to blatantly breaking the local laws.

That gave me a bit of concern for our own libation adventures. We had to be somewhat careful. More notes to self, "Don't blow up your alcohol".

Buck was gone, and now Murray was in charge, but not for long. We were assigned a new sheriff, and he would arrive very soon. Man, we hoped the next guy was better than Tribuck. I couldn't imagine how it could have been worse.

Chapter 55
SHIT

Months ago, when we first arrived at the fire department on the flight line, we were given an area to occupy. It had a garage area, kind of like a small truck bay, and a makeshift bunk room at the far end, so if you walked through the garage doors and straight back you go through a door into our sleeping area. The outside of the building was made of a sheet metal material. A radio room sat to the left inside, and also the bathroom.

I've seen some bad bathrooms in my day. Plenty of the roadside, gas station bathrooms looked and smelled about as bad as one can imagine. However, when our Saudi friends showed us the bathroom they used, the only thing we had to say was, "no fucking way."

It seems that in some cultures, like this one, the shower stall is the same place you also take a poop. The people in many countries are famous for squatting all of the time. Instead of standing around, they just squat, and when it comes to pooping, they just put an extra large hole in the floor of the shower and squat.

I'm all for different cultures having different ways of doing things, but as firemen, especially a military firemen, we're made to keep our trucks, our building, and ourselves clean, dry, and serviceable. We wash, mop and scrub everything, nearly every single day, to keep it as clean as it is able to be. When we were shown our toilet at the fire department, we were a bit put off.

One day, while in the bunk room, we noticed the undeniable whiff of shit in the air. Had someone cut loose a particularly aromatic intestinal burp? This particular smell did not go away, and in fact, became more intense. As you walked to one side of the room, the degree of smell became nearly unbearable. One of the cots against the wall was pulled away, and we noticed an unmistakable brown color seeping under the wall.

Shower + Toilet.

It was pure, unfiltered, straight from the sewer, shit.
In our bunk room.
Where we sleep.
And it was coming under the wall at an alarming rate.
We pulled back the carpet to expose the truth of the disaster.
Gallons of liquid sludge had made its way into our little room. Upon inspection, we determined the shower/toilet was on the opposite side of the wall and something had obviously gone wrong.

It wasn't like anyone was coming to help us out of this shitty mess. This was going to be just another stupid job in the long line of ridiculous things we had to do since we arrived. We pulled up the carpet, found a shovel and pail, and started shoveling.

Shoveling shit.

One of the guys remembered we had some *speedy dry* we used to soak up fuel spills. It's a glorified kitty litter. He pulled some off the truck and began applying it to the sludge. Now we had something with a delightful consistency to scoop up. Lovely.

We made sure the plumbers were notified so that we didn't end up scooping shit for the rest of our stay here. Eventually, we had the mess taken care of. We had to pull up all of the carpet in the entire room to throw it away. Several cans of Lysol later, the smell was gone and we hoped the problem was too.

No one wanted to use the bunk next to the wall anymore.

Ya just can't make this shit up.

Chapter 56
Brief Rewind

My first duty base in the Air Force was R.A.F. Chicksands. The R.A.F." stands for Royal Air Force, as in England, the Queen, Big 3en, and fish-n-chips. American military are stationed on these eased bases.

Good for England. Good for the Yanks.

I was there for two years, from 1987 through the spring of 1989. highly recommend it.

The interesting about this particular Air Force Base is that it didn't have a flight line. Yup, no runways and no airplanes.

What kind of Air Force Base has no airplanes, you ask? This base was set up with a big-ass, super huge, round antenna. It looked like a gigantic cage, and hence became known as "the elephant cage". I'm not sure where the "elephant" part came from. People in England drink a lot, so anything can happen.

After being there over a year, I was due for some training, and someone decided that Airman White needed to go to *rescue school.* That sounded fun to me, but what was even better was that it was in Germany. I would be there for two weeks, learning rescue shit. Sounded like a paid vacation to me. I like vacations, especially when someone else is flipping the bill. Thanks America!

Off I went, not really knowing what was in store for me there. I couldn't be bothered with too many details. Put me on a plane, tell me where to go, and I was good.

Once I got there, I discovered one interesting fact. At least half of this class was going to be devoted to intense training on how to enter several different types of aircraft, then shut them down and extract the crew and passengers. I had not seen a military aircraft since firefighter school, about eighteen months ago, and that was some very, very basic training. Most, if not all of the people in this class with me were at bases that had airplanes of some type or another. They trained on them weekly. I was well behind the learning curve here. When we had classes about the aircraft, they would use terms and speak about situations I just hadn't had the opportunity of confronting.

Not only was I behind on the aircraft knowledge, but all of the different kinds of fire trucks that were used for fighting aircraft fires. The differences between those trucks and the ones to fight building fires were vastly different. They operated completely differently, and the tactics used to fight the fires were also completely different. I also had very little knowledge of how to conduct myself on a flight line. There were procedures for entering a taxiway and runway I was completely clueless about. I was a fish out of water here, and I was not enjoying it.

But I powered through the two weeks of training. I studied, asked questions, and tried to absorb everything I could. Most of it was loads of fun. It was hard, but I enjoyed the challenge.

What concerned me more than anything was why I was even here. The rescue team back at Chicksands was well-established. These guys were never going to give up their spots, and I didn't see them leaving anytime soon, so I had no expectation of ever being on that truck. My base didn't have any airplanes, so all of the cool skills I was learning here were going to go to waste. Even if my next base did have aircraft, I'd be so out of practice, it would be like starting over again.

Eventually, I just decided that this was going to be a fun vacation. The weekend between the two training weeks left me time to travel and see the nearby country. I took some trains to nearby towns, ate good food, drank great beer, and chalked this up to a cool adventure. There was no way in hell that I'd get to use much of my newly learned skills, but really, I wasn't fighting many fires either, so mostly, I was just enjoying myself and having fun. I had joined the Air Force to have experiences, see the world, and put some life under my belt. That's exactly what I was doing.

Who knew that one day, I'd find myself in a war in the desert? Ain't life a hoot?

Chapter 57
New Chief, New Life

Master Sergeant Raymond Wulliez showed up out of the blue to take control of our lives. Honestly, Murray was doing a stellar job, but the folks with bigger brains and higher rank decided that Ray was needed. He seemed like a nice enough guy, and for the first few shifts, we were all feeling each other out. He wasn't sure what he just got dropped into, and we didn't know if he was friend or foe. We had just gone through Buck and were a little leery of those at the top. They could make this go smoothly or be a nuisance to our efforts in so many things. We would find out soon enough.

Up until now, Mike Long had been the Crew Chief of the rescue truck on my shift. Mike was a nice enough guy, but he was certainly eating up the prestige of being the top dog on the rescue truck. Some people who obtained higher rank or status were able to maintain an air of grace and humility and not throw their privileges in the faces of their fellow workers.

This was not Mike.

He made sure you knew he had this thing to hold over you, and everyone else. He could come and go as he pleased, and do whatever the hell he felt like, because he was in charge of RESCUE.

Whatever dude.

I had a shit ton of wine back at my house and you are at my mercy to have one little sip.

Then Wulliez hit the door. He had no ties or reasons to play favorites with any of his new troops. After a few days of getting his bearings, he had some announcements to make. He wanted to make sure everyone who was in their current positions was qualified to be there.

He started with this one, simple question, "Who here has been to Rescue School?"

As I raised my hand, I saw the fucked look on Mike's face. He wasn't raising his hand.

Rut Row.

In fact, out of the entire group of firemen, only two of us had raised our hands. Two, and I was one of them. He looked at my name tag, since he didn't know my name yet, "Sgt. White, you'll be Crew Chief on A Shift, and Other Dude, you'll be Crew Chief on B Shift." Then he continued with the other trucks and other crew chiefs. He didn't even stop to recognize the giant shift in power that just took place. Maybe he knew, maybe he didn't. I wish I would have asked him later.

Holy shit balls.

Mike looked at me like this was *my* doing, but I was too shocked to really know what the hell just happened. I had just gone from mid-to-lower totem pole to the guy in charge of the mother fucking rescue truck.

Extra holy shit balls!

Not only had I never been any part of any rescue team EVER, but now I was in charge of the whole shebang. My stomach left my body, and went on vacation somewhere, and I'm pretty sure all of the blood just drained out of my face. My palms were sweaty. I felt fucked, and not in the good way where the condoms came out to play.

Tom and I had come to be pretty good friends over the last several weeks. After several roof parties of getting trashed together, we had gotten to know one another pretty well. He also knew that Mike was an arrogant ass for no good reason. When Tom walked up to me with a grin on his face, I knew he was getting a little kick out of this. I think he saw the look on my face and was getting a clue to what was going on in my head.

"So, who do you want on your crew with you?" he asked.

What? I didn't see that coming.

Since I was in charge, I got to pick my own crew. The only sensible answer was to keep Cowboy and Archabold (Arch) on the crew. They already knew the ins-and-outs of this operation, so to start from scratch would be crazy. One thing was for sure, Jim needed a shit ton of refreshers, and these two poor guys were in for the ride with me.

Chapter 58
Catch up

I walked over to Mike and collected the rescue radio from him, which he wore proudly on his belt. I wonder if he thought I might pick him to be on the team, but that would have been too weird. He would have been second-guessing my decisions, and trying to run the show. If I was going to be in charge of this team, I was going to do it my way.

I just said, "Sorry, dude," and walked over to Cowboy and Arch. Time to put our heads together.

We walked over to the rescue truck, and I said, "OK, here's the deal. I've never been on a rescue team so we need to get out there and train on every airplane we can find. I know you've done this with Mike but now we need to make sure I'm up to speed so we can do this and not look stupid."

I was trying to sound like I had a plan.

"Cowboy, are you cool staying the driver and Arch, are you okay still being in the back seat?"

They both agreed. These guys were great and I couldn't have asked for two better guys for a rescue crew. I think they were a little shocked by all of this as well and had decided to just do the best they could with what just got thrown into their laps. I was completely untested in this role and I could either make this shitty or make this great. I decided we were going to train our asses off but have as much fun as possible doing it.

Our base was primarily the home of the AWACS aircraft, those big airplanes with the huge, spinning bowl on top. They are so weird but amazing to look at. They were constantly taking off and landing just outside our fire department doors. However, our base was also the base that was far enough away from the action that about every other type of aircraft came to our base to refuel and let the crews rest and have something to eat.

If you aren't familiar with all of the different kinds of planes the military has, I won't bore you with all of their special names, but there were several. Not just Air Force planes either, we had every branch's aircraft landing and taking off here.

Know what that meant? It meant the rescue team was responsible for knowing how to enter each aircraft, shut it down, and remove all people.

Did I know how to do that? Nope.

My base at Eaker AFB had two kinds of airplanes, and since I wasn't on the rescue team, all I needed to know how to do was throw water and foam on them until they weren't on fire anymore. I was so far behind the knowledge curve here, it was staggering.

Did Wulliez have any idea how lame his new Rescue Crew Chief was? I had to think not, because this was crazy. It was going to take me several shifts just to bring myself up to "adequate."

Once I gathered my team I said, "We are going to get on every airplane we can find and make sure we are all on the same page. I want both of you to get a notebook you can carry in your pocket. We are going out to each airplane and write down every step to get in, shut down, and pull out the crew. Okay?"

They both agreed and actually seemed excited. That was good because I didn't want them pissed off about all the extra work we were going to be doing over the next several shifts.

There were too many planes to train on in one day, but I figured if we could get to two or three a day, we should be in good shape. I said, "If we see a plane land that we've never trained on, we'll go out and try to get the pilot or crew to let us train on it." Again, they sounded like they were excited to do this. Hey, it was fun to get on different airplanes and see what they looked like, right? Jet fighters and cargo planes and everything in between. If we weren't lucky enough to get to fly in these cool planes, at least we could play on them.

For the remainder of our tour, this is exactly what happened. We went to all the aircraft making Riyadh their home base, or just stopping in for a quick visit. If it was a large plane, I'd find the crew chief and say, "Hi, I'm Sergeant White with the rescue crew. We'd like to look at your aircraft so we can rescue the crew in case of an emergency."

This was a great opening line. I wanted them to feel like we were there to actually save *their* asses if there was a crash or fire.

It was a hard thing to say "no" to. In fact, most of the time, the person would then proceed to take us on a tour of their aircraft, showing us every way possible to make entry. We also asked them to show us how to shut down all of the engines, activate any onboard fire suppression systems, and how the belt restraints worked so we could extract everyone.

All the time, the three of us were writing in our notebooks, making diagrams, and double-checking each other to make sure we knew who would be doing what. We would run through the procedure a few times, then go back to our truck and finish our notes. We would discuss any questions we had with each other to make sure we were all on the same page.

If it was a small jet, I'd do the same thing with the pilot. Sometimes, the pilot would let us sit in his seat so we could see where everything in the cockpit was. We would also make sure he (we didn't encounter any female pilots) would show us how to *not* activate the ejection seat. Setting off an ejection seat on the ground would be a bad day for everyone. Sitting in the pilot's seat of an F-16 or other jets is way, super cool, even on the ground going zero miles per hour. I loved my new job.

One of the aircraft we were allowed on was a brand new JSTAR airplane. This was a top secret plane that was an upgrade to the AWACS plane. It was a big plane and when it landed, I had no idea what it was. It had a huge pod on the bottom, but to me, it was just another plane to say I was on. I had my little speech ready for the crew chief as soon as the engines died down.

He looked me up and down kind of suspiciously and said, "Okay, but this plane doesn't exist. I'll let you on and show you how to shut it down and remove the crew, but as I take you through the plane, don't look at anything, and if you do see something, forget you saw it." The three of us looked at each other and were barely able to hold back the smiles.

This sounded cool already.

We went to the cockpit and did our usual stuff, then he walked us through the rear of the plane. It was filled with all kinds of stations on both sides. Many of the crew were still there, looking at all kinds of screens and doing stuff. I mean, uh, we looked straight ahead and saw nothing……..NOTHING!

Truthfully, I had no idea what the hell I was even seeing. It was just a bunch of high tech computer-looking stuff, but it didn't make a lick of sense. It was hard to "not look" at all of the stuff as we walked down the center. When we were done, the crew chief took us outside and gave us each an arm patch for this particular airplane.

Wow! I had an arm patch for a nonexistent, top-secret airplane! Did I say I loved this job?

The other remarkable aircraft that landed was the U-2 spy plane. One day, this sleek little black plane zipped down from the skies and landed.

Oh, shit.

I wanted to have a look inside this historic plane.

It didn't taxi back to the pad with all of the other aircraft, it remained parked at the end of the runway, well away from everyone and everything else. That didn't stop us from driving out. As we approached, we could see the pilot getting into a black SUV and driving away, but another guy was standing nearby, so we got out of our truck and approached him. I gave him my routine speech and expected him to be happy to comply.

Nope. Not this guy.

He was stone-faced and said, "If this plane crashes and is on fire, you are not to approach it. If that pilot can't get out himself, then he doesn't get out."

He just stared at us, and I really didn't have a reply to that except, "Really?"

All he said was, "Yes."

The U-2 spy plane was not going to be put into our little notebooks. We drove away, feeling bummed. The next day, the plane zoomed down the runway, and as soon as it was airborne, it went straight up like a rocket, to the cheers of everyone who witnessed it.

U-S-A! U-S-A! Incredible.

Chapter 59
Happy Holidays

Christmas and New Year's were soon upon us. These particular holidays for military people far from home can really suck. It's those special times that families really pull together and soak it all up.

Presents passed out. Decorated trees. Kids excited.

The end of a year. You put that last year behind you and set your goals on new stuff.

But being away, sitting in a desert, away from your family, puts your life in limbo. Those moments are gone. It can be depressing if you let it.

Lucky for me, this group was determined to make sure we didn't feel too much of these ill effects. We hunkered down and had ourselves a knock-down-drag-out, super roof party. We made sure we had plenty of wine, food, music and decorations. No stupid war was going to get this group depressed.

We threw caution to the wind and invited everyone we knew. After getting to know our new fire chief, we discovered he was our kind of people, and invited him, too.

The fire pit was rocking, the grill was smoking, the music was jamming, and the wine was sloshing.

We even broke out the unfiltered wine, but had to strain it through some pantyhose to get out the sludge. No one seemed to complain.

How could anyone bitch about free wine and food?

We never asked our guests for money. We just threw big-ass parties and had a good time. What the hell else did we have to spend our money on?

The Twister game was in full force and pants went flying off. Goodbye, 1990, and hello, 1991!

We knew we were days away from the final "line in the sand." Saddam had barely three weeks left to get the hell out of Kuwait. After that, none of us knew what would really happen.

Would he haul ass north?

Would he actually try to fight us?

You could tell everyone was letting completely go and turning a corner. This crazy group was going to face something together in a few days, so this giant party was going to be an end of one thing and a beginning of another.

Let's hope Sgt. Grim Reaper Pennington didn't know what the hell he was talking about.

Happy New Year! Cowboy and Dunc.

Chapter 60
I'm In Charge?

I was having a blast being the Crew Chief of the rescue team. After I had a few weeks under my belt and we had practiced our skills over and over, I began to chill out and enjoy the role. We were a good team, good friends, and had each other's back. During my stint in the Air Force, I had rarely been in charge of anything. I was crew chief of different fire trucks now and then, but it was more of a fill-in capacity. When I got this job, and eventually felt confident in our abilities as a team, it felt right. I began to think I might even be good at this job, and wondered what would happen when I returned to my base in Arkansas. I wasn't very hopeful, but I left that thought to linger for another day.

While I felt better about the job, it wasn't until we had an actual emergency on an aircraft that I began to get the idea that other people might believe in me and my team. One afternoon while we were working, we got the call that a C-5 was having an inflight emergency. A C-5 is the largest cargo aircraft in the US Air Force. Both the nose and the tail sections hinge upwards, so cargo can enter or exit from both directions. It's so large, it fits several tanks, or even helicopters inside.

It's a monster.

At the moment, one was about to land at our base, and the crew was reporting smoke in the cockpit. That's not a good sign.

The fire department was dispatched, so we all saddled up into our trucks and sped off to the flight line to position ourselves and wait for the flaming bird to make its arrival. As Cowboy, Arch, and I sat waiting for the plane, we each got out our notebooks and reviewed our procedures for the C-5. By the time the tower called to announce that the aircraft was on final approach, we were ready to rock. Arch and I put our air packs on so we could bust out quickly if need be. Cowboy had to wait since he was the driver and it was mpossible to drive while wearing the air pack. The rest of the fire rucks were positioned at points on the runway so we could quickly espond no matter where the plane stopped. It was a well-rehearsed dance.

We would see the plane from miles away. This thing was so big and lumbering, there was just no missing it. It seemed to defy gravity as you watched it.

Nothing that large had any business in the sky.

We took out our binoculars to get a better look. There didn't appear to be any smoke coming from the outside, a good sign, but he crew was still reporting smoke inside. The tower announced that as soon as the plane landed, it would come to a stop and the crew would immediately exit. I guess they didn't want to stick around while their plane burst into flames. I didn't blame them.

Finally, the plane touched down, screamed to the other end of he runway and came to a stop. All of the fire trucks gave chase as soon as the plane passed their position, and so did we. As our rucks surrounded the plane and pointed their water turrets towards he aircraft, we could hear the engines begin to shut down. Cowboy, Arch and I got out of our truck and began to walk towards he plane as we saw some of the crew begin to come out of the side door. They informed us that the pilot was still inside shutting down the rest of the plane. There was still smoke in the cockpit, but no fire. That was all good news.

Then it got interesting. Our good friend and assistant chief, Tom, showed up to see what we were thinking. I looked over at Tom and asked, "Ok, what do ya want to do?"

Tom gave the briefest of smiles, looked at me and said, "You're he Rescue Crew Chief, this is your scene, you're in charge. Tell everyone where you want them."

Then he just looked at me.

Really?

He just put me in charge of a $200 million dollar aircraft, and all of the fire crews?

Cowboy and Arch just looked back and forth from Tom to me, waiting for someone to say something.

Fuck.

I felt like this was a fun little test Tom was giving me, so I just went with it. "Have all of the crews hold position around the aircraft Cowboy, Arch and I will make entry and try to find the source of the smoke."

I waited for Tom to give me some input, but he just said, "Okay."

That was it. I guess I wasn't doing anything wrong, at least, not yet. I told Arch to grab a halon fire extinguisher, just in case, and we walked up to the airplane. Holy crap! This thing is a monster of an airplane.

We climbed the ladder to get to the cavern of the cargo bay. We didn't encounter any smoke here. Time to climb again. The way up to the cockpit was by a ladder from the cargo bay. You had to go up several stories to the door. We were in full bunker gear, with air packs, so the climb wasn't easy, especially with those big rubber boots. We didn't have our masks on, so that was a plus. Eventually we made it to the top and came up through the floor into the crew area. The crew area in a C-5 is way more than just the cockpit. Since this plane can theoretically stay airborne until they run out of food, the crew could be in the air for hours, or even days. There is a bunk area, bathroom, shower and kitchen. It's small but probably larger than some New York apartments.

We met the pilot at the top. He had just finished shutting down the aircraft. We asked him to describe what happened and where he thought the smoke might be coming from. It was his plane, so he would have had the best idea where the problem might be. He said it smelled like an electrical fire but since the plane was so large and had so much wiring, it was anyone's guess where it might be coming from. The instrument panels in the cockpit didn't indicate any trouble areas so that was no help pinpointing the trouble area. Because the door had been opened to let the crew out and us in, the smell had dissipated so much we had no way to find out where it was stronger.

I told the guys to split up and walk around the aircraft to see if they could see or smell anything, but since the plane was shut down, I wasn't very hopeful. I updated Tom on the radio as to what we were up to so the rest of the crews had some clue as to what was going on. I knew that sitting in a firetruck waiting for the Rescue Crew to do "their thing" can wear on your patience, so I wanted to keep everyone informed.

It took us most of twenty minutes of walking around, looking in every place we could find, or the places the pilot told us to look. It was like searching an apartment complex.

Finally, we gave up.

The smell had gone away and there just wasn't any way to track down the problem. I was also aware that no aircraft could land on this runway while we sat here, which wasn't a good thing. The only solution was to fire up the engines and taxi this thing to a parking pad. If the problem started again, we could track it down then.

I told Tom my plan. I would stay in the cockpit with the pilot and the halon extinguisher while the pilot taxied the plane. All of the fire trucks would follow and be ready in case something exploded.

Tom just said, "10-4."

He was really just letting me do whatever the hell I thought was best. This was a whole new level of trust and responsibility that I had never experienced before. Maybe this padawan was about to be a Jedi soon. Was the FORCE with me?

I've got to admit, being in a C-5 cockpit as it taxied around the flight line was an experience and a treat I'll never forget. It was like being in a sideways building as it drove around. You are so far up in the air as the plane drives around, it's hard to describe. It just didn't seem possible. As the pilot maneuvered back to the parking pad, we kept waiting for the smell to return. I updated Tom a couple of times that the smoke hadn't come back. Finally, we came to a stop and again, the pilot shut down the engines. We exited together and I returned to my truck to finally take off my air-pack and bunkers. This had taken about two hours and I was glad to get out of this getup. Now it was time for the mechanics to figure out the problem.

We didn't fight any fires or save any lives that day, but something had changed.

I had changed.

My boss had trusted me with a level of responsibility that I had never been given before.

Sure, it was my job to do this stuff, but up to that point, I had never been tested. It was a good dry run for anything that might happen down the road. I seemed to have made the right decisions, and didn't screw anything up, so all good stuff. This single event changed my life forever. It showed me I was able to be responsible for important things. I could actually handle being in charge of people, equipment, and events. It would be a lesson that would shape my future. Thank you, Yoda. I mean, thank you, Tom.

Chapter 61
1991

In the early weeks of 1991, life began to change. January 16th was the last day Saddam had to pack up his camels and go back to the cave he was born in. We were told that anytime we left our houses, we had to take our chemical warfare gear with us. If we went to the gym (a converted house) or MWR, or to visit a friend in another house, we had to lug around a bag with all of our gear. This included our gas masks, charcoal lined pants, charcoal lined jacket, rubber boots and rubber gloves. It was very fashionable.

The 16th came and went, and on the morning of January 17, the US stopped with the sanctions and proposals and gibberish. They put their missiles where their mouths were and sent several tons of whoop-ass raining down on the Iraqis.

It was a sight to see, and see it we did.

Everyone had CNN tuned in as we watched a war happen live.

It was weird to watch a war happen in real time on television. No one had ever seen anything like it before, or since. Reporters were camped out in apartments in Baghdad, broadcasting bombs dropping and missiles blasting as anti-aircraft fire streamed like fire hoses into the night sky.

The shit had finally hit the fan, but as far as we were concerned, we felt a bit removed in Riyadh. We were several hundred miles to the south of the action. We had heard of Saddam's S.C.U.D. missiles, but there was wild speculation as to if they could reach us this far away. There were also questions as to their accuracy. Would he just be lobbing them at the entire city, hoping they would eventually hit something or anything at all? There were debates as to if he could put chemical weapons on the S.C.U.D.s and get them to fly as far as Riyadh.

No one wanted to test the theory by not having their chem warfare suits ready. We had seen the gruesome videos in Basic

Training of what even a dot of chemicals could do to a person and most would rather be dead than suffer through that. It didn't take long for us to find out many answers to our looming questions. Shit, meet fan.

Chapter 62
Pucker Factor

On day four of the war, which had officially been changed from Desert *Shield,* to Desert *Storm,* I was working at the fire department. Since getting the rescue crew chief gig, I worked exclusively at the flight line fire department. For the last three nights, Saddam had fired his S.C.U.D.s at Israel and Dhahran. He would usually fire them after midnight, for some unknown reason. Seconds after each missile launch, our radios would announce the event, after which we would hold our collective breaths and wait for them to next announce what direction and therefore, what city was the target. We had been lucky so far. Maybe he didn't want to waste them on Riyadh.

It's important to realize just where the fire department is situated to get a feel for what happened next. The fire department building sat on one of the minor taxiways of the airport. If you walked straight out of the fire department garage doors, you had to watch for vehicle traffic, as well as the small trainer jets that would also come and go. These small trainer jets were kept under an overhang just about fifty yards in front of our building. After the tiny jet overhang, there was a large bit of land before you reached the actual taxiway.

It was this sandy area before the taxiway that several PATRIOT Phased Array Tracking Radar to Intercept On Target) missile batteries were deployed, each holding four PATRIOT missiles. They looked like long boxes pointed towards the sky. They were about 200 yards from our front door. Beyond that was the major taxiway the large aircraft would use, and then the actual runway. A fire department needs to be as close to the flight line as possible so if an emergency occurs, we can be there lickety split.

So on day four, just after midnight, we were still all wide awake, waiting to hear if there would be another attack. We were all in the truck bay area of the fire department, kind of like an extra-large garage area. Suddenly, the radio came to life and announced, "We have multiple missile launches, standby."

Some of the Patriot Missile launchers pointed towards Iraq.

My palms instantly began to sweat.

It seemed the radio guy was taking a extra few seconds to make the next announcement.

"We have confirmed inbound towards Riyadh."

Even he sounded a bit surprised.

It felt like some kind of dream, or like I was having a stroke. My mind immediately went into a kind of overdrive, like when you fall off your bike and realize you have zero control over what happens next. My blood pressure must have shot through the roof instantly. My heart took off, and my stomach dropped. All of this happened in about two seconds.

I felt sick.

There were nine of us standing there, and as I looked at them, we were all suddenly frozen, our eyes as big as saucers, mouths hanging open.

FUCK TIMES A MILLION!

We had less than ten minutes to prepare to be bombed.

Suddenly, it was assholes and elbows!

All you could hear were the zippers of people ripping open their duffel bags to pull out their chemical warfare suits. They were ripping open the sealed pouches of the suits, something we had never, *ever* had to do before. We had all practiced with old shitty, used suits to see how it all worked, but this was the first time we had broken the seal on a brand new, never used, suit.

This meant it was the real fucking deal.

Shit! Shit! Shit!

We had practiced and trained for this countless times, but never when our heart rates were balls through the roof. Just basic things like operating a zipper suddenly become a complicated task.

Tick, Tick, Tick.

This was taking way too long. It felt like the seconds of my life were ticking away.

Why couldn't I get this fucking suit on faster?!

Some put the pants on first, some put the shirt on first. A few put the stupid mask on first, making *everything else* impossible to put on. We started trying to help each other, but as we were talking, everything came out as screams.

Fuck!

We were completely out of control.

Finally, we were able to get everyone outfitted in time, but then someone felt like the areas where our gloves met our suits was a place the evil chemicals might get in. I grabbed some duct tape and started taping up my arms, and then the area where my boots met my pants. Suddenly, everyone was doing it.

Rip! Riiiip! Riiiiiiiiiiiiip!

All you could hear was the ripping of duct tape for the next couple of minutes. This would have looked hilarious for anyone watching, except for us feeling like we were about to die.

With what felt like seconds to go, Tom yelled, "Everyone into the bunk room!!!!" We didn't know why, but we all ran in and closed the door.

Why were we in the bunk room?
Was it a better room to die in than the bay?
Were we actually hiding from the S.C.U.D.s?

Then the sirens started, like air raid sirens from old WWII movies. Everyone was silent, not knowing what to expect next. Except for the sirens, all I could hear was my heartbeat in my ears and the breathing in this stupid mask. Is this how Darth Vader felt all the time? We were all just standing in this little room, waiting to see what happened next.

If you've never been 200 yards from where a missile launches, you're missing out. You don't just hear it launch, you can feel it in every molecule of your body. The pressure in the air changes. The sound is exhilarating and terrifying at the same time.

The entire building shook with the horrific rumble, then there was a second launch seconds later.

Then a third, and before another one, there was a massive explosion over our heads.

Not skipping a beat, more and more PATRIOTs began blasting off. Then more explosions over us again.

Suddenly I realized I was screaming, and between breaths, I could tell everyone else in the room was screaming, too. Between screams were just good 'ole "MOTHERFUCKER" and "FUCK, FUCK, FUCK!!!!!".

You didn't know what to do.

Hiding under a bunk wasn't going to help you.

Standing around like an idiot seemed wrong, too.

There just didn't seem like a good way not to die.

After each explosion, which seemed to be a few hundred feet directly over our heads, the entire building would shake. It shook when a PATRIOT launched, it shook when the S.C.U.D. exploded. Why and how the glass in the windows wasn't exploding with each concussion, I'll never explain. It felt as if the whole building should just collapse. I could picture people sifting through the wreckage of this building, looking for our dead bodies later. Happy thoughts! Happy thoughts!

It just kept going on and on and on.

How many fucking S.C.U.D.s did this dick shoot at us?

We kept hearing bits of metal hit the tin roof over our heads as pieces from the explosions rained down. There was absolutely nothing I could do to save myself from dying. The feeling of total helplessness was overwhelming. Either a big chunk of a missile was going to fall on us and crush us, or not.

The official number of PATRIOTs launched was 26. It was believed there were only four S.C.U.D.s Multiple PATRIOTs were launched at each S.C.U.D., but if that's what it took to save our asses, I was all for it.

Launch 100 for each one for all I cared! Pay the bill later.

Just keep my happy ass in one piece.

After the explosions finally stopped, all we could hear were the sirens again. Suddenly, someone started whooping in their gas mask. They were happy to be alive. We all started whooping!

Pennington was wrong today. All ten of us were still alive.

I grabbed my camera from the gear bag on my bed and told everyone to get up against the wall for a picture!

WE SURVIVED! FUCK YOU, SADDAM-FUCKING-GOAT-BALL-LICKING-HUSSEIN!

I have never before, and never since, had that much adrenaline running through my veins as I did during those few minutes. It's not an experience I wish to repeat.

Eventually, someone tested several areas around the base to detect if there had been any chemicals released during the explosions. The tests came back negative, and we were finally able to take off our masks and suits. We needed to kill this bastard quick, because I never wanted to go through that bullshit again. That didn't happen, but we no longer took any chances and made some big changes, fast.

Survived our first S.C.U.D. attack.

Chapter 63
New Plan

The potential for an entire shift of the fire department to die all at once was quickly realized, and acted upon immediately. Gone were our twenty-four hour shifts. Gone was working out of the fire department.

It was time to put the new plan into action.

We were now going to work twelve hour shifts. Instead of working out of the fire department, each crew would disperse to their assigned revetment. They would park their truck in their hiding hole, and hang around their revetment area. If there was an attack, we would jump onto our personal hiding holes and wait for death and destruction to rain down from above.

Hey, it was a plan.

But what if there was an aircraft emergency, and we had to act like firemen? They had these new rules too.

Listen closely, because this is what is *supposed* to happen. Most of our aircraft emergencies are actually declared while the airplane is coming in for a landing. Something usually goes wrong with the airplane, and the pilot calls to let the tower and firemen know what the situation is. Sometimes they smell smoke. Sometimes something has gone wrong with the landing gear. In any case, as soon as we get the word, we would normally jump into our fire trucks and haul ass to the runway and wait for the plane to land (or crash), then deal with whatever we had.

Our new procedure is as follows. We were to wait until the aircraft was within five minutes of landing, then, and *only* then, were we to get in our trucks and drive to the runway. It gave us fewer chances to get caught in a S.C.U.D. attack while not at our revetment. Perfect plan. Right?

Roll call was now at 7am and 7pm. If you were coming to work, you would leave Eskan Village just after 6am on a school bus, with

your trusty chem gear bag in tow. We would get to ELF1 area just before 7am and wait for the guys from the revetments to drive back to the fire station. We would do a quick roll call, pass on any information, and then switch
places. The guys who had been at the revetments the last twelve hours would load back into the bus and go home. The rest of us would head out to our revetments. This was our life now, and I've got to tell you, it really cut into our roof time.

My schedule was from 7pm to 7am, the night shift. This ended up being a great deal of fun, but it was also when all of the attacks happened. Now if we wanted to have a little sip, and we did, this was what life looked like.

Take bus ride home and arrive back about 8am.

Find the nearest wine bottle, open said bottle, and start drinking immediately. Hey, don't judge. We were all doing this.

We'd flip on the television and watch CNN for the latest and greatest news on what shenanigans were happening to us. After getting mildly shit-faced, we go into our rooms, where we had garbage bags taped over the windows to block out the sun, and get a few hours of sleep. Because we were on the night shift, we didn't really need that many hours of sleep, because we took shifts sleeping at the revetments. This left more time for wine when we got home. We had this down to a science.

For some unknown reason, we even outfitted our living room in wartime fashion. We hung the camo netting from the ceiling, and with the mandatory addition of duct tape on the windows for explosions, it was a fine looking place to live and party. As time went on, a couple of us actually went to the gym immediately after getting home. We'd do a super quick workout, and *then* get to the wine. We were still brewing and bottling this entire time too. Nothing ever got in the way of that. Nothing.

The ultimate wartime bachelor pad!

Chapter 64
Midnight Festivities

I was never much of a night person. My internal clock just wasn't set up that way. But now I was forced to watch the sun go down, and then up again during every shift. I began to see things I'd never taken the time to notice. Watching the stars slowly rotate over your head was an amazing spectacle. Every evening, I'd watch the same stars rise, then travel across the sky. Every night they would shift just ever so slightly. I began to understand how sailors and early observers could navigate with these constellations to point their way.

Saddam would also break up the evening. For the next month, we'd get fairly regular S.C.U.D. attacks. The second one was nearly as frightening as the first one. Our rescue crew revetment was near the end of the runway, fairly close to the mail depot (where all of the incoming mail was delivered). I was answering one of the several letters from people back home when the radio gave it's announcement, "S.C.U.D. missile launch has been detected, standby...."

We waited to see where they thought it was heading.

The radio chirped back up, "S.C.U.D. tracking towards Riyadh, take shelter at this time."

The sirens would begin to blare, and once again it was a mad dash to get all of our shit on as fast as possible. When we each thought we had our suits and masks on correctly, I made us check each other to make sure nothing was missed. We'd stand in front of each other and spin around, letting the other two guys see if we had the suit on correctly and if we had missed taping up anything. You didn't get two attempts to get this right.

You did it right or you died.

When we decided we were good, we crawled through the hole into our little bomb shelter, and waited. All you can hear in those ucking masks is the sound of your own breath, or your heartbeat. Soon, the wait is over, and the scary, awesome PATRIOT missiles begin blasting off.

Over the next several minutes, all that could be heard was the deafening sounds of nearby rockets launching into the sky, and then seconds later, the explosions overhead. Sometimes the explosion sounded a mile away, and sometimes it sounded like it was right over our heads. We could feel the plywood roof shake while the sand and dust sifted down through the cracks.

The very air vibrated and pounded you.

If this were the Fourth of July, we'd be excited to be this close to the action, but this particular action was trying to kill us.

Not so fun.

On and on it went, and you kept wondering how long we could be lucky not to have some heaping piece of a missile come falling on our little shelter. I didn't think the plywood was strong enough to withstand a direct hit. Our odds of survival seemed to melt away with every PATRIOT that roared into the sky. All we could do was stare at each other and wait to live or wait to die.

It was thirty PATRIOT missile launches and several S.C.U.D.s later, the "all clear" was finally announced. Again, we had to wait for people to check for chemicals.

This time, it came back positive.

MotherFUCKER!

We just sat in our shelter and continued to wait. Man, I hoped all of this shit I was wearing really worked. For the next hour, they did more tests. Finally, it was decided the first test was a false positive, and no chemicals had been used. Later, it was determined that someone's OFF bug spray had contaminated one of the tests. Who knew?

We crawled out of our bunker and looked around. Except for a few Security Forces vehicles racing around the flight line with their lights on, nothing looked out of place. A few minutes later, one of the security vehicles pulled up to check on us. They looked a bit freaked out. I don't think they had made it to a shelter. One of the guys pulls out a box with several pieces of metal, freshly hot and twisted. He told us they were pieces of one of the S.C.U.D.s that blew up. I asked if I could have a piece, and he reluctantly parted with one.

I still have that piece of metal to this day.

After this attack, things got more interesting.

Chapter 65
ChanWhitelyDunc

Being attacked by the camel jockeys (oh, I am *so* far from politically correct"), from the north had an interesting effect on how he world viewed the troops. We were already being highly supported, but now the support for our efforts skyrocketed.

One way to say thank you was to send us beer. They couldn't send us real beer, because alcoholic drinks in the Kingdom was ighly illegal. Not wanting to start an international incident, the fine people at the Miller Brewing Company decided to send cases, and ases and pallets and airplanes full of non-alcoholic Sharps beer. m not sure they realized what would happen next.

Maybe they did. Wink. Wink.

We were told we could each collect a case of Sharps beer at a pecific location. Every two weeks, we would be able to do this again. I had never heard of Sharps beer, and the thought of non-alcoholic beer did not entice me in the least. However, one of our British friends had heard about this development, and gave us ome valuable, top secret, information.

He had the recipe for turning this worthless crap in a can into the oldest known beverage known to mankind: beer.

We were stunned. You could turn *near* beer into real beer? Why idn't I know this when I was 17?!

This was like when Indiana Jones discovered where the Holy Grail was hidden. Was this some myth? Could it actually be done? was ridiculously simple.

Each of the firemen collected their case of fake beer and then rought them to our house. In order to do this magic trick, you eeded several cases of beer at a time. We now had several ases. In fact, we told other people that if they donated their beer to s, we would give half of it back to them in a much different form. Many agreed. It was a fair deal.

Give us your water-beer, and in a few weeks, we will return half of it as real beer, and for the effort, we keep the other half. No one complained.

The new company "ChanWhitelyDunc" (our combined names) was formed. All we needed to make this work was a brand-new, plastic garbage can, lots of bottled water, sugar, and the magic fairy dust, commonly known as yeast. Our British friend gave us the directions, and we immediately made a beeline to the local grocery store for supplies. We were becoming "regulars." By the end of the day, we had the mixture fermenting.

Surprisingly, our entire house now smelled like a bread factory.

It was hilarious, but at the same time, we were sure the smell would instantly give away exactly what was going on. We sure as hell weren't baking bread.

By this time, we had so many upper brass as drinking buddies, we had let our guard down a bit on being overly careful. People were too busy with the war to care about some firemen making a few gallons of brew.

At least, that's what we told ourselves. Denial is a wonderful state.

All we had to do was put some plastic tightly over the top of the can and put a small hole in the top so the gas could vent. Easy peasy, right? When the mixture stopped bubbling in a few weeks, we would transfer it to bottles with a little more sugar, and then a week or two later, beer. Yes, this first batch would take a while, but good things were worth waiting for, plus, we were still heavy into the winemaking, so all was good.

Step 1: Pour beer, water, sugar and yeast into garbage can.

Step 2: Weeks later, siphon beer into bottles with sugar.

Chapter 66
Bullshit

On our next shift at our revetment, Tom decided that he needed to have a home bunker to hang out at, and ours was the one he picked.

We arrived just after 7pm and Tom inspected our bomb shelter. We mentioned that the sad, thin, plywood roof didn't have a snowball's chance in Saudi Arabia of stopping more than a sixth-grade girl from jumping on it.

That was unacceptable.

Our solution came in the luck of where our little shelter was situated, near the mail intake building. It wasn't really a building so much as a huge, temporary hangar-like structure. The aircraft would arrive with pallets of mail, offload the mail to the hangar, then trucks would drive it to locations in Saudi Arabia or deliver it locally to us.

Here is the important bit. These were not the good 'ole wooden pallets most people were used to seeing. These pallets were one-inch thick, metal pallets, and much larger than their wooden counterparts. Several empty pallets were stacked a few feet from our bomb shelter, not a good use for them, as far as we were concerned. These pallets needed to be *liberated.* It didn't take a lot of imagination to what we did next, but we had to do it fast. Night was coming, and that was when the S.C.U.D.s came calling.

We quickly disassembled the roof of our shelter. We removed all of the cool looking radar-evading, camo netting. Then we threw all of the sandbags off to the side and took the flimsy-ass plywood off and tossed it to the side. We went to pick up the metal pallet. We couldn't.

It wasn't just heavy, it was *super,* fucking heavy.

It would make an awesome roof if we could only move it. We needed to liberate a forklift!

Eventually, by pushing and sliding and grunting, we got this thing into place, but it was a job. Just before the sun finally set, we had the sandbags back in place and our netting on top. No one at the mail depot seemed to mind, or care. Maybe they just didn't see us. We were working on the "don't ask permission, ask forgiveness" method.

Okay, let that evil bastard try to kill us now.

No. Not really.

We didn't know if this would really make a difference, but at least we knew we had done all we possibly could. Let that sixth grade girl jump on it now.

Chapter 67
Brave vs Stupid Part 1

As we sat around our little revetment, we needed things to do to pass the time. You can get a lot done in twelve hours, or you can be bored to tears. I always brought two or three letters from people back home with me. They were random letters from kids at schools or just nice people writing to keep our spirits up. I wrote all of them back. I wanted to give them some idea of what life was like here, and to thank them for thinking of us. Everyone won.

We also found an abandoned, slightly broken wheelbarrow near the mail depot. We pushed it over to the front of our bunker and christened it the Rescue Fire Pit. All we needed was an endless supply of wood, which, thanks to our friends at the depot again, were all to happy to oblige.

Actually, we never really asked.

In fact, we learned to never ask for anything.

Just *liberate* things when we needed them, and if somehow we made a mistake, then we would make an effort to repatriate the item or items. That rarely happened, but that was what we would use if asked. We would gather the wooden pallets that appeared to be haphazardly thrown aside, grab our trusty fireman's axe, and begin to make some wheelbarrow firewood. Whack! Whack! Whack! Every night, we would blaze up the wheelbarrow, stare into the fire, and talk about the world. And we would wait.

Wait for the attack.

It rarely disappointed us.

As the attacks continued, we became less terrified, then not so scared, and later, kind of brave.

Brave is probably the wrong word.

Stupid is probably the correct word.

Forrest Gump said, "Stupid is as stupid does," and we were certainly doing stupid things.

Me and Tom. Marshmallows over wheelbarrow. Waiting for S.C.U.D.s

I had begun bringing out my radio/cassette player to the
revetment to play some music at night. In the spirit of documenting
the entire clusterfuck, I not only tried to take loads of pictures, but I
had also decided to record our S.C.U.D. attacks. If we survived this,
might be cool to listen to later. Right?

During the second S.C.U.D. attack, as the sirens blared their
warning for us to suit up and jump into our hiding holes, I placed a
new cassette tape into the radio and hit the record button. If the
radio survived the attack, then the recording would be a cool
momento. Later, when we got the all clear and wiggled back out of
the bunker, I replayed the recording. It worked!

As we began to have more trust in the PATRIOTs never missing
the S.C.U.D.s, and no one at Riyadh being hurt, most everyone
stopped being afraid. In fact, it now became somewhat of a
fireworks display. Once the sirens would begin, we would put on
the last of our chem gear and just stand near the door/hole to our
bunker. If you looked around the flight line, most everyone within
eyeshot was doing this, too. We would see the fire behind the slow-

moving S.C.U.D.s as they approached from the north. We would wait and watch the PATRIOTs blast into the sky.

It was spectacular to watch multiple rockets launching.

You could feel the air vibrate.

We would watch as they zoomed upward, looking for their prey. When they eventually hit the S.C.U.D., it was like the Fourth of July times one hundred. Only then, when a S.C.U.D. was hit, and we were sure the debris was raining down, did we scurry into our bunker and wait for the chunks to stop falling. Eventually, after several attacks, the people in charge got wind of everyone standing around during the attacks, instead of immediately hiding in holes. They were not pleased.

We were ordered to cut that shit out, and protect ourselves, for God's sake.

We didn't see these idiots at our revetment, so we continued to do as we pleased.

We always knew better.

Chapter 68
Brave vs Stupid Part 2
The Dunc Chronicle

I'm sorry there isn't an audio accompaniment to this book, because while the story of what happened next is very funny, there is an actual audio tape as well, and it would leave you in tears. Remember our procedure for in-flight emergencies while in our war mode living at our revetments? We dreaded this actually happening because if you were to have a S.C.U.D. attack while wearing your S.C.B.A. (self-contained breathing apparatus) firefighter air pack, you could be potentially screwed. Those air packs, at the time, were only good for about thirty minutes. It was a closed system, just like a SCUBA diver, or an astronaut. You were only breathing what was in the bottle on your back.

You would think this would be the ideal way to go through a S.C.U.D. attack, too, except for a few problems. Sometimes we would be in our chem warfare masks for well over an hour during attacks. The attacks were over quickly, but it sometimes took over an hour to confirm there were no chemicals used. While it was possible to do emergency bottle exchanges without removing your fireman's air mask, it wasn't a practical or long-term solution. You could stay in a chem mask for hours and hours. You could actually drink water (or whatever is in your canteen) while in your chem mask. They had designed a little tube you could manipulate to hook up to your canteen, and then move it so it would rotate to your mouth on the inside of the mask. It wasn't easy, but it worked. The fireman's mask couldn't do that. That was one of many good reasons to not be having a fire emergency during a SCUD emergency.

But the odds finally caught up to us. One of our firemen was a larger fellow who may or may not have been pushing the limits of scale capacity for a military member. His nickname was Koala, not because he may have looked somewhat like a Koala Bear (he did), but it somewhat matched how his last name appeared.

Remember how people would shout, "Norm!", on *Cheers* when that character walked into a room? People here would shout "CO WALL Ahhhhhhhhhhhhhh" and hold the "ahhhhhhhhhhh" as long as possible. Sometimes we would do it all together. It was funny shit.

During one particular evening, each of the crews were enjoying the night sky at their revetments. Dunc and Koala were in a large P 4 truck by themselves, parked smack dab in the middle of the runway sand, very, very close to several PATRIOT launchers.

And then it happened.

We were told that there was an in-flight emergency on an incoming C-130 aircraft. It was still about twenty minutes from landing. The rest of us did what we were supposed to do.

We waited.

In fifteen minutes, we would jump into our trucks and head to the flight line to deal with the plane as it landed. We were practically on the runway already, so it wouldn't be a long drive to begin with. The rescue team was ready.

Dunc decided on a *Dunc Plan*. He was the crew chief of this truck, and made the command decision to drive out to the edge of the runway and wait for the plane as soon as the emergency was announced. They jumped in their big, lumbering fire truck and drove a few hundred yards to position themselves accordingly. While waiting, Dunc pulled out his micro-recorder that he used to make tapes to send home, instead of writing letters. He was sitting back in his seat, feet up on the dashboard, recording his letter, when we suddenly came under attack, without prior warning. All anyone heard was the sirens suddenly going off.

HOLY FUCK! WORSE NIGHTMARE SCENARIO!

For those of us who stuck to the plan, we put on our masks and jumped into our revetment bunker. Dunc and Koala were screwed.

They had a single instant to decide whether to drive back to their revetment, or to bail out and start running.

They went with Plan B.

Both were smart enough to put their gas masks on immediately before leaping out of their truck and start sprinting back to their bunker, but they didn't even get close. Within steps out of the truck, the PATRIOTs began blasting off. If the enormous, explosive launch was an incredible thing to experience hundreds of yards away, Dunc and Koala were getting it a hundred fold, as they were a stone's throw away from the launchers. Dunc had stuffed his tape recorder into his flak jacket before he jumped out of the truck. He had left it on "voice-activated", so as long as it heard sound, it kept recording, and since things got very noisy very fast, it recorded the next several minutes of the entire attack.

The first thing you hear is Dunc scream, "OH, SHIT!", as the first PATRIOT blasts off, and Koala, who was running beside him yells, "FUCK!". They were running in dry sand, so they weren't making great progress, but they were highly motivated, to say the least.

Then you hear the sirens as they are both sucking air, trying to set a land speed record while wearing gas masks. For the next minute, all you can hear is heavy breathing as they are running, the sirens blaring, PATRIOT after PATRIOT blasting off and the explosions over their heads. There is nothing more *war zone* than what they were experiencing. Bombs exploding hundreds of feet over your head and metal raining down around you is about as terrifying as it gets, and they were getting it all. They didn't know it, but the concussions alone had already knocked over the camo netting on their revetment they were so desperately trying to get back to.

Suddenly, you can tell their surroundings have changed from the muffled sounds of the sirens. They had made it to their bunker and had shot inside the little entry hole. They both continue breathing harder than it seems their masks will allow air to filter in. They are just trying to catch their breaths.

Finally, between breaths, Dunc manages to blurt out, ".....you all right, Koala?!"

All he could reply with was more heaving breathing and moaning.

Dunc must have been concerned now because he repeats, "Are you all right?!". Finally, through more heavy breathing Koala gets out, "I'm all right, man."

More sirens blaring in the distance. Then Koala catches his breath just enough to ask Dunc, "You okay?"

"Yeah, man," Dunc gets back out.

Then Dunc, his brain beginning to realize what just happened says, "Oh, fuck!"

To which Koala gives back a, "Motherfucker!", still trying to breathe.

Then Dunc starts laughing loudly and hysterically, happy to be alive, and burning off the ten gallons of adrenaline pumping through every fiber of his being.

Dunc says, "Our truck is out there man!",

"What?" Koala replies, like he can't believe the statement.

Dunc says again, "OUR TRUCK!"

"Fuck the truck!" Koala classically replies, still gasping for every breath.

This must have amused Dunc, because he began his high-pitched hysterical laughing again. More calmly, Dunc asks Koala if he is all right, clearly hearing how hard he is still breathing.

Koala just says, "I need air", and the tape ends with the sound of both of them trying to catch their breath in those stupid masks.

After that incident, we had to review our emergency procedures to ensure something like this didn't happen again. On our bus ride home, Dunc played the entire tape for us as I held it up to my radio and recorded it for myself. I've listened to it several times over the years, and it never gets old and always makes me laugh. Living on the edge of dying gives you some new perspectives, and makes ife's little problems fade to the background. Don't sweat the small stuff, as they say.

Chapter 69
A Taste of Home

When you are this far removed from your normal life, you almost begin to forget what it was like. The day-to-day little things that you don't think about.

The car you drive.

Your favorite places to shop.

Sorting through the mail or saying "hi" to the same people that you run into a few times a week.

You begin to take these little comforts for granted. But when they are gone, you realize a large chunk of your life has been removed. It's almost like you are physically missing part of yourself.

Then a funny thing starts to happen. Those things, and the memories of those things begin to slip away. They start to get replaced by what's happening to you now on a day-to-day basis. When you are in a temporary arrangement like this one, that can be a sad thing, and it can become a dangerous thing.

One of the things we seemed to always talk about was the food we missed and the places we liked to eat. It usually started out with, "When I get back I'm going to eat...," and then a favorite food or restaurant would be named. One of the foods that reminded me of home more than anything else was Skyline Chili. If you aren't from the area around Cincinnati, there is a type of chili you won't find anywhere else in the USA or the world. It was developed by Greek immigrants around World War II. There's just no describing it unless you've had the privilege of tasting it. It's served in combination with spaghetti and cheese, and can have additional toppings of onions and beans. You order it by asking for a "three-way" or "four-way", or even a "five-way", depending on how many toppings you like.

Nothing said home to me like smelling or tasting some of this chili. When my mom asked me if I wanted anything special sent, it was easy to answer.

One day, I got a package from home. My wonderful mom had finally sent the much anticipated Skyline Chili. For weeks, I had been trying to explain how awesome Skyline was to my fellow firefighters, but knew there was only one way they would be able to understand my culinary ramblings. They had to taste it for themselves. I almost felt sorry for them. Once they allowed their deprived taste buds to finally experience this mecca of delight, they could only long for the day they might make their way to Pig Town, USA to once again enjoy what I could have on a daily basis if I desired. Poor bastards.

As I opened the box, I discovered several cans of the chili, along with some dry, boxed spaghetti. The first chance I was able, I went to the market to get some onions and cheese. I was gonna treat everyone to some heavenly piece of home. I invited my shift from work over to the house and began preparing our lunch. I boiled my water, and got my noodles going as I warmed up the cans of chili. I cut up the onions and put out some shredded cheese. Once people began to smell the chili, I had lots of help in the kitchen. The noodles couldn't cook fast enough.

Finally, the moment arrived. I gathered everyone in our little kitchen and showed them how to build their three-ways. This isn't just like putting spaghetti and sauce on a plate.

Oh no, no, no.

This had to be done just right to achieve the proper balance in order to finally eat it properly.

First, you put the noodles on the plate, not in a bowl. Not too many, but not too few.

Then you add the chili on top. Cincinnati chili isn't extremely thick, so you have to ladle it out to cover the noodles.

Next, if you are so inclined, and if you have them available, you add the onions, and/or beans.

Finally comes the shredded cheese. In chili parlors back home, no one skimps on the cheese. It is put on in such a large, heavenly mound that you look at it in disbelief, wondering if anyone should be eating that much cheese in one sitting. But don't fear, once you begin eating it, the sense of the entire entree begins to come together. It's the perfect balance of tastes, brought together to form a picture of home.

To eat this chili, you use a fork.

Only a fork.

Not a fork and a spoon.

You use the edge of the fork to cut off chunks from the ends, trying to get spaghetti, chili and cheese together with each forkful. If you are lucky enough to have oyster crackers at hand, you can add these in any manner that makes sense to you. Some put them strategically on top of the cheese. Some just eat them between bites. Also, a hot sauce of some sort can be doused on the cheese if you feel the need. Personal preferences can become an art form.

All I had to do was cut off that first bite, lift it to my mouth, close my eyes and take a bite.

I was back home.

Sitting at the chili parlor.

Iced tea ready to drink.

The rattle of plates and silverware being collected from abandoned tables. People talking to each other about the Reds or Bengals.

I wanted to hold on to that part of my brain for just a second, to let me be overwhelmed by this thing that transported me far, far away. I must have looked like an idiot. Smile on my face, with my eyes closed just a bit too long, slowly chewing this magical gift. I looked around to gauge how my friends were enjoying this unworldly pleasure. For the most part, everyone agreed it was a interesting and good meal, but I could tell they didn't get it. I couldn't blame them though.

This wasn't from their home. This didn't remind them of another place. They had no fond memories associated with its smell or taste. It didn't matter. Until the last bite, I had my few moments of home.

Then I missed it again.

Murray, Dunc, Cow, Koala and myself, having a treat from home.

Chapter 70
Cowboy Rides into the Sunset

For the last few weeks, Cowboy was dealing with a situation back home in Arkansas. He had a sick family member, and things didn't look so good. Cowboy and the military agreed that being home was more important than what we were doing here, so orders were given to send him packing. Getting out of this sandbox was a mixed bag for everyone. Going home was a good thing. Why he was going home was a sad thing. We had all bonded together in a unique way that most people will never know. Looking into the eyes of the guy next to you when you fully expect to die any second can turn friends into lifelong buddies, brothers even. It's not something we knew would happen as we flew here so many months ago.

The fire department was losing a valuable asset. A guy who could turn a shit situation into something we could not only tolerate but have fun doing and laugh along the way. Those kinds of people don't come along very often. The entire dynamic of our little band of misfits was about to change. We were happy for one of us being able to leave, and a little lost knowing that some of the glue holding us together was about to disappear. I was also losing one of my rescue crew. We were a great team and worked perfectly together. I wasn't sure we would, or could, find a suitable replacement.

With all of his shit packed, we said our goodbyes and watched our friend get into a truck to head to his plane for America. It was surreal to think that in just a few hours, he would be home. America had almost become an idea now. It didn't seem possible that one day we would be able to leave this place. Living there was almost like a weird jail that we had become so accustomed to, we were unsure what the real world was like or how to behave once we got back to it. Working twelve-hour shifts, living in the sand, hiding in holes, drinking too much, making alcohol, and being in this weird land had become our new normal. We had just given into it so we didn't go crazy, and now the thought of America just didn't seem possible sometimes.

Now Cowboy was about to find out.

It was obvious he was sadly excited to be leaving. He was partially responsible for helping to build this new lifestyle that we could bear, and he was going to miss it.

And then in the blink of an eye, Cowboy was gone.

Chapter 71
Enter Puddin

Baby, here I am
I'm the man on the scene
I can give you what you want
But you gotta' come home with me...
-The Black Crowes

Cowboy's replacement was Jim McPadden, henceforth to be known as *Puddin.* Back at Eaker, we were on opposite shifts, so I didn't get to know him very well. Maybe Jonesy and Drew were holding me back. As soon as Puddin stepped off the plane, Dunc and I whisked him back to the house to make sure we in-processed him properly. We threw his bags on the floor, and before the dust settled, we were on the roof opening several bottles of wine.

We may have overdone the "welcome to the war" party.

Hey, it was important to let Puddin know right from the beginning what our priorities were, and what this war was all about. He fit in perfectly, from the first hour.

During the next shift at the fire department, it was decided that Puddin would make an excellent replacement for Cowboy on the rescue team. We immediately set out to take him around to every aircraft we had previously been to so he could make his own notebook, and give us a refresher. It was a crazy blessing to have someone immediately fit in so perfectly. Puddin had the exact personality that anyone needs to step into the middle of an ongoing, fucked-up situation. He had a zen-type quality about himself I soon realized was missing from my own life and needed to incorporate. There was no doubt that he was a fun-loving, hard-partying, crazy-ass dude, but he also had an inner peace that most of us never are able to realize.

Puddin also changed the mood of the group as well. Where I had us on the soundtrack of *China Beach*, he brought us a new tape from a group I had never heard of, the Black Crowes. I had

Puddin's "WELCOME TO THE WAR"

We may have overdone it. By 10am.

never heard music like that before, but now I was digging it, and the mix of the two tapes became the background music of our lives.

Mellow China Beach and rocking bluesy Black Crowes.

The entire vibe of the roof changed as well. Cowboy had set the wheels in motion for our party, and Puddin came in and greased them up again. He also was well-versed in the ways of making contacts which suddenly turned our world for a new and exciting spin.

Puddin had skills.

Mad skills.

Chapter 72
CNN is Trying to KILL US!

Most mornings, after we had spent the night at the revetment getting attacked, we would come back to our house and flip on the television. CNN would be showing video footage of our attack, and the reporters would be giving comments. It was pretty cool to see the same attack on TV that we had just survived of a few hours ago.

What a crazy way to go through a war.

But one morning the reporter must have lost his fucking mind.

As we all grabbed a glass of wine and settled on the couch to watch the latest episode of *Days of Our Lives: Desert Storm Edition*, we couldn't believe what we were seeing and hearing. There was a reporter standing on a balcony in downtown Riyadh. He was giving a description of the attack he witnessed a few hours ago. However, as he began describing where the PATRIOTs intercepted the S.C.U.D.s, he also began to tell *exactly* how far and what direction the S.C.U.D.s should have aimed to hit strategic targets.

He was telling the fucking enemy how to correct their last attack to better kill us the next time.

This motherfucker was telling dickwad Saddam Hussein, who was certainly watching CNN, where to point his missiles tonight.

What the *fuck* was this guy thinking?!?

Had he just lost his fucking mind?!?

We were all screaming at the television for this guy to somehow shut his fucking pie hole. Wasn't there a producer or director or anybody to shut this guy down?!

Holy shit balls!

This guy needed to be told to stop this bullshit, and to stop it *right fucking now.*

I had an idea.

I got out my AT&T calling card and called the operator in the USA. I asked to be connected to CNN Headquarters. The CNN operator answered and asked how to direct my call? Fuck! I hadn't thought this through. Who the hell do I ask for? I didn't know how a giant ass-newsroom was put together. I wanted the boss or someone in charge, but who is that?

I tried to explain my situation without sounding like a lunatic.

"Look", I said, "I'm in Riyadh, Saudi Arabia. The guy on the news just gave out information about how to get us killed, and he needs to stop. Who do I need to talk to, to make sure he gets told to stop giving the enemy our location?!"

Did I just sound crazy?

All the lady could say was, "Hold please."

Several minutes went by listening to stupid recorded commercials on how awesome CNN was. When I say "minutes went by" I mean "lots of my money went by." Calling card calls to the US were a pay-by-the-minute deal and I had heard the same commercials enough times to feel the money flying out of my wallet. I was beginning to wonder if my bank account could survive being on hold much longer.

Everyone in the room was standing around me, waiting to hear what would happen next. Finally, a man came on the line, "Can I help you?", but he said it in a way that I was pretty sure he didn't want to help me at all.

"Sir", I said, hoping by showing a little respect, I might appeal to his senses. "I'm stationed in Riyadh and just watched one of your reporters (I actually gave him the reporter's name) give very detailed information as to exactly where Saddam needs to shoot his missiles to hit the targets he missed last night."

As much as I was trying not to yell, I'm pretty sure I was technically yelling. At some random guy stuck with answering phones in the CNN newsroom.

I didn't want to come off as crazy, but I'm pretty sure I was doing exactly that. "Would you either take that guy off the air or tell him to stop saying stuff like that because he's going to get us killed over here!"

Yeah, I was definitely yelling.

Was I even talking to someone in charge? This could have been the janitor for all I knew.

All I got was a, "We'll look into it."

That's it?

That was it.

All I could say was, "Please do so, thank you".

What a crazy-ass war. We drank more wine. Fuckwad.

Chapter 73
I Love Surprises!

The war had been raging on for a few weeks. We were firmly settled into our new normal.

Come to work, roll call, drive out to revetment, do shit for the next twelve hours to make the time pass by. I would write my letters, watch the stars slowly march from east to west, and talk to the guys while keeping the fire going in the wheelbarrow. Sometimes Saud would come by with food to throw on our makeshift grill to have a little desert cookout. If we were lucky, Saddam would try to kill us and we would have a nice fireworks display. See how ridiculous our new normal became?

We also took turns taking naps in the bunker hole. One at a time, we would go into the bunker for a two or three-hour nap if we wanted one. We rarely got a full eight hours of sleep during the day since that cut into our roof time festivities. We had our priorities. The other guys would hang by the fire, listen to the radio, and alert the sleeping guy if there were incoming S.C.U.D.s. We had built benches inside our bunker to sit/sleep on, so while it wasn't a bed at the Hilton, it was better than a dirt floor.

One night, while it was my turn for a nap, I was in a nice, deep, bunker sleep. I felt someone shake my shoulder, so when I opened my eyes, I expected to see one of the guys letting me know it was their turn for a nap.

It was Mary!

Was I still asleep and having an awesome dream? How could Mary be in my bunker? She was in Dhahran. Right?

My brain was still trying to put all of this together as I was only half-awake. She just looked down on me and smiled like an angel. She was *really here!*

I sat up and said, "Holy crap! How did you get here?!?"

"We just flew down on a mission, so I went to the fire department looking for you, but they said you were at your evetment, so Saud drove me out here," she said.

I was blown away and amazed. "I only have a couple of hours until we leave," she said. A few hours of Mary were better than none! We hugged and traded a few smooches, then crawled back out of the bunker.

I found Saud and Sadik and shook their hands. What a cool gesture. They could have just turned her away, but they took the time to drive her to see me. We all stood around the fire, talking about her short visit and when we might see each other again. Her missions to Riyadh were usually last-second flights, so there was no way to know when or if she would do this again. I just counted my blessings that she was here at all.

Life was good. Mary was a keeper. Soon it was time for her to join her crew for the flight back to Dharan. Saud and Sadik drove her back to her plane. Goodbyes sucked.

Chapter 74
Wine and Beer and Sid, OH MY!

After much anticipation, our first batch of beer was finally ready to drink. We had bottled it and waited the proper amount of time for it to reach minimum drinkability. Now we were in business.

Or so we thought.

With beer and wine came an interesting development. It seemed that some enterprising British military dudes had set up quite an operation to make "moonshine." In Saudi Arabia, "moonshine" is called SIDIKI (Sa-Deek-ee), or "SID" for short. A new relationship was forged.

One day, Puddin brings a liter water bottle to us, but the liquid inside isn't quite as clear as water, and in fact, had a few "floaties" inside. By the large smile on his face, I knew we were about to hear an interesting tale. It seems that Puddin had formed a wartime alliance with some British firemen. While they were set up to make large quantities of SID with their a wartime still, they did not have access to beer and wine. While we could buy some SID outright from them, they preferred a trade. If we would provide them with beer and wine, they would, in turn, provide us with SID. Everyone wins. Wartime allies are the best. We were our own NATO but we were concerned with the free and fair booze exchange.

And with that nifty arrangement, life was complete. Our parties now took on a full-fledged, Animal House quality. Beer, wine, and mixed drinks were in full demand, and fully available. The music got louder, and the craziness became more extreme.

Our entire lives were like some crazy television sitcom. I didn't think anyone back home would believe the things that were taking place.

Get attacked at night, then come home and watch it on television as we got shit-faced on homemade beer, wine and moonshine we traded with the Brits. We would fire up the grill, play music, and have fun with the girls.

This was war?

This was Desert Storm, fire department style.

But the war was still in our way. There were two thoughts to the war ending. First, if the war ended, we could get our night time rooftop parties back to full throttle and once again enjoy ourselves with the reckless abandon to which we had grown accustomed. Second, if the war ended, we would soon go home, thus ending our new and carefree lifestyles.

It was a tough situation.

We all wanted to go home yesterday, but we were having a good time, too. To go home meant to rejoin reality. Bills. Daily routine. Failing relationships. In the end, we pretty much all agreed that going home was the best outcome, but no one doubted that we would miss this little slice of war we had made for ourselves. But the party wasn't over yet, and we still had plenty of crazy shit to do.

The Hamel Camel

Chapter 75
You Did What?!

If it weren't for the pictures, I doubt anyone would believe what we did/accomplished next. Remember the large, heavy, black, water-holding containers we used while building tent city? They were made out of thick rubber, and weighed several hundred pounds. Their intended purpose was to hold water so it could be piped to showers.

We found a better solution.

While in a somewhat inebriated state during one of our many daytime parties, someone mentioned it would be nice to have a hot tub on the roof.

We had a grill and games; why not a hot tub?

Why not, indeed.

Someone suggested there were several water containers not being used at the moment and one of those would make an outstanding hot tub. The conversation soon turned to other topics, and it was forgotten by all, except for one person.

A couple of days later, we received a knock on our door. It was Murray, and he was wearing a particularly large, shit eatin' grin on his face.

"Come see what I've got," he said, as we followed him outside to his pickup truck. He stopped at the rear of the truck, turned and smiled. We looked in the bed of the truck, and there it was, a rolled up water container.

We looked back at Murray, and caught ourselves before we asked the obvious question.

Don't ask questions you don't want answers to.

Answers will only put you deeper into a hole. Best to remain clueless.

Besides, it was obvious that this container was in need of being liberated, so we were only assisting in its freedom. That's why we were here in the first place, right? Freedom. (Oil, cough, cough, wink, wink).

We put the tailgate down and a couple of us gave the container a pull, but it didn't budge. A few more tried to help, but it was obvious that it would take as many people as we had to get this object out of this truck. Six of us were able to pull and lift it out of the truck and to the front of the house, but we discovered that there was no way in hell we were going to be able to bend and twist this thing up two flights of stairs and up to the roof.

But we were not beat. We were Americans, dammit. If we wanted a hot tub on our military housing roof in the desert in the middle of a war, we were going to make it happen. We devised a plan.

Being firemen, we had access to several different and helpful tools that might assist someone who is determined to move a half-ton of thick rubber on to a walled roof, twenty feet in the air.

Rope. We needed rope and we quickly located several hundred feet of rope to tie around the middle of the rolled-up rubber tub. We left this at the bottom of the wall on one side of the house.

We took the rope up the wall and completely across the roof to the other side of the house, where we threw the other end of the rope over the wall to Murray, who was standing at the bottom. Murray took the free end of the rope and tied it to the front of his pickup truck, where a tow hitch was conveniently positioned. Murray is sitting in the truck, ready to drive backward at a high rate of speed when given the word.

Puddin and I are on the roof to make sure the package actually makes it to the roof.

Others are positioned on the ground and near the truck to relay info to Murray. What could possibly go wrong?

It all looked like it *should* work. We gave the thumbs-up and relayed for Murray to go. He put it in reverse and stepped on the gas.

Nothing happened.

It was too much weight.

Murray was not discouraged. Before we could discuss our next option, Murray put the truck in neutral, revved up the engine and slammed it into reverse. The truck immediately shot backward at a ridiculous rate of speed, across the street and barely missing a fire hydrant. As the truck shot backward, the rope pulled the rubber bladder up the wall much faster than anyone anticipated. As it reached the top of the wall, it flew several feet into the air.

Not good.

We had a rubber bladder weighing hundreds of pounds flying through the air across our roof.

In a split second, I saw the problem.

I instantly imagined the bladder hitting the opposite wall, but instead of going up and back over, it was going to go through the wall.

Shit on a stick!

Without realizing it, I started yelling at Puddin, "STOPPPPPPPP!!!!", hoping he could relay this to Murray in the half second it was going to take to make this clusterfuck somehow uncluster itself. By some miracle, Murray stopped backing up and the bladder slammed to the ground and skidded to a stop at the bottom of the opposite wall. Holy shit! That was close.

After everyone's heart slowed down and we stopped laughing, we had to decide where to set up our potential hot tub. Once set up and filled, it could easily weigh close to a ton, so we couldn't just put it just anywhere on the roof. We went back inside the house and found where two load-bearing walls intersected, then went back to the roof and measured the same distances to figure out where to center the tub.

We may be reckless, drunk, or hungover, but we weren't stupid.

There would be no way to explain how a thousand-gallon water retention tub fell through our roof and destroyed an entire house. We centered the tub and began to set it up.

Over the next few days, we built a floor for the tub because we needed to run PVC pipes in order to blow air bubbles and to recirculate the water for filtering. When the air and water pumps were attached (yes, we liberated those as well), all we needed was the water. Easy peasy, since we were firemen. We had access to hoses and the tools to connect it to a nearby fire hydrant, one almost recently demolished by a freak accident involving a truck and a flying bladder. We ran the fire hose from the hydrant, across the street, into our yard, through the front door, up the stairs, and into our hot tub. Eventually, we had a fireman's version of a hot tub on a roof in Saudi Arabia during a war. You've got to make due with what you have.

Yes, I took lots of pictures of this entire event. Enjoy.

Waiting to be pulled up.

Rope across roof, ready to pull up the tub.

Where it eventually came to a stop.

Setting up THE TUB

Fire hose across street so we can fill THE TUB

Running the hose up stairwell to the roof.

Filling the tub. Hoping it isn't downstairs soon.

Chapter 76
Fastest War EVER

As I told you at the start of this tale, I'm not going to give you a very historical accounting of the war. Suffice it to say, forty-two days after war was declared, and one hundred hours after the ground war started, the entire thing was over. No sooner than we were told the war was over than we began asking when we could go home.

Absolutely no one would tell us.

All they could say was that people from home would eventually come to rotate in to take our places, but that could take weeks or months. *Months*?

War or no war, all of the things that we were protecting as firemen still needed to be protected. Aircraft, buildings and people. All of these things just didn't go away as soon as the war was declared over, so as long as those things existed, the firemen were needed. Crap.

I was already nearly two months beyond my four-year enlistment, and I had places to go and things to do. Eventually, I relaxed and realized that I was at the mercy of the largest ball of red tape in history, so just go with the flow and chill out.

And there was no better way to chill out than with a nice beverage.

Now that the war was over, and we could convince those in charge that we were all safe and sound, we went back to our normal fireman work schedule. Yahoooooo!

Twenty-four hours on, twenty-four hours off, and if all went well and Saddam behaved himself, we might see the 'ole "kelly day" again.

This meant one thing: The party machine was turned up to full-speed ahead.

The coals on the grill never had a chance to get cold from that day forward. Wine and beer were brewing at 100% capacity. We were no longer mixing SID with anything, as we had become so accustomed to it we were drinking it straight from the bottle. The music was loud, the roof games were rocking, and the parties kept getting wilder and larger by the week.

We could tell our days here were growing short, so we needed to squeeze every crazy moment out of it that we could. We made it through this long-ass buildup and survived the entire war, contrary to Pennington's declaration so many months ago.

We were going to blow this popsicle stand to pieces and eventually put this camel farm in our mirrors.

Wreckless abandon was our new mantra.

Party all night, work off a hangover the next day as we attempted to survive at the fire department and start the party all over again as soon as we got home.

It was a weird and surreal way to live, but there really was no other or better way to do it. We were making some memories here, and they were going to be epic.

Getting in the last parties.

Everything is funny drinking S.I.D.

We survived a war together. Take THAT Pennington!

Chapter 77
Goodbye, Farewell, So Long

Nearly as quickly as we were told to grab our bags and get on a plane to come to this sandbox, we got the word we were going home.

Numb.

I felt completely numb.

It just didn't seem true or possible.

Leave? It was such a mixed bag of emotions, I was stunned.

I'd never felt so many things so instantaneously in my life. Relief and sadness and joy and dread and excited and scared. As fucked up as this was, I had become so accustomed and comfortable with this way of life, I wasn't sure exactly how I would act when I got home. I was no longer scared of rockets blasting off as they tried to intercept missiles trying to kill me. I was used to the idea of going into a city where there were terrorists plotting to kill me. We partied like New Year's Eve every other night. We made alcohol by the gallons weekly and sold some of it on a black market for even more alcohol.

I hadn't seen grass in months or smelled that wonderful aroma that it gave off just after being cut. No bills to pay. All normal responsibilities suspended. This was almost worse than coming here in the first place. Talk about a fucked up head.

But there we were, one day before leaving, bags packed and ready to go. Our new friends at the Saudi fire department on the flight line wanted to give us a goodbye sendoff. They put tables in the fire bay and ordered loads and loads of sweets.

It was a great gesture from our new friends.

We all got dressed up in the best clothes we had and went to our party. I just kept looking around, realizing that I'd never be here again, or see this place. This place that had been my home, my bomb shelter, and my workplace for the last several months.

Not all of us were going home though. My group from Arkansas were the first to arrive, so we were the first to leave. Our friends who came later, Puddin included, were here for several more weeks or months. It felt weird leaving them behind. We had survived this ordeal together, so we should be leaving together, but the military has its own ideas. Truthfully, they needed experienced people to stay behind to show the incoming people what to do and how to do it. Not to mention, that beer and wine wasn't going to bottle itself.

During these last few weeks, Puddin had actually begun to ramp up quite an alliance with the SID brewers, and after we departed, he turned it into a large enterprise. He has a good head for business.

Loads of cake and cookies. It was like an 8-year-old's birthday party!

Our Saudi friends saying goodbye.

Chapter 78
Not How To Travel
Part 1

When we had first arrived in Saudi, our load of M-16s was taken out of the crates and stored for us at the armory. The crates were then thrown away. Now we were leaving, and we had to take our rifles back home with us and no crates for them.

We had to carry them. Our first flight was all military people on a chartered commercial jet, which didn't present a problem. Our rifles were handed to us the night before we left.

No ammunition.

Not even the magazines to hold the ammunition.

Basically, we were given expensive, cool looking metal clubs to take home. Being firemen, who rarely had the chance to play with, I mean, train with guns, we decided to take loads of pictures of ourselves looking cool. We looked stupid.

Best War Picture EVER! Hahaha!

The next day, we boarded a bus to Al Kharj to catch our flight.

Why were we driving nearly two hours to a airport when we had a perfectly good one twenty minutes away?

If you start asking questions like this you undermine the entire U.S. military.

Just best to let it go.

Before we were allowed on the bus, they wanted to scare the shit out of us one last time. We exited the bus and saw a tent and fence between us and the flight line. To get to the plane, we would have to go through the tent. That seemed odd. As we walked towards the tent, there was a large sign which read *amnesty tent*. For the most part, it said, "Hey idiots: If you have *anything* on your person or in your bags that is illegal to have or transport back to the United States, you have this one last chance to throw it away. While inside the tent, there is a box. Throw any contraband into the box, no questions asked. If you come out the other side of the tent and we find anything on your person or in your bags, we will arrest you immediately."

Okay, that got my attention.

Why? Because I had a bottle of SID in my pants that I thought might be a nice momento to bring home. I took my turn and stepped into the tent. Sure enough, there was a large box with a hole to let you slide items into.

I peered into the hole. There were several large items already inside, most of which were knives, but I'm sure I saw a few guns and possibly explosives. Was that a hand grenade? I took out my bottle of SID, pondered taking a big swig, but instead just dropped in into the box.

A sad way to start a trip.

After we each took our turns entering and exiting the tent, we walked to a building to wait for our plane. Our bags were collected to be put on a pallet, but we held on to the guns.

And we waited.

We waited ten hours.

Why in the sam hell had we left so early from the comfort of our nice homes with beds, to sit in this shitty building for ten hours, waiting for a plane?

Ahhhh yes, more "military."

I could already tell our travel plans were going to be some fly-by-night clusterfuck.

I wasn't disappointed.

Chapter 79
How Not to Travel
Part 2

We boarded our chartered plane just after midnight. This time we were in normal aircraft seats instead of sideways ones made of straps. That was a definite upgrade. Two and a half hours later landed in Cairo, Egypt. This would have been an awesome place for a long layover, as the tourist in me wanted to see some pyramids and the Sphinx, but because it was dark and we didn't even leave the plane for the two hours we were on the ground, I didn't see anything but the airport from the window.
It's not a very impressive view.

Off into the night sky we went again, and this time we landed at 7:20am local time in Shannon, Ireland. We had a two hour and twenty minute layover here as well, but this one was more to our liking.

We had to get off the plane and wait in the terminal. We must have looked pretty beat up and sad by now, because the first thing we saw in the terminal was a bar. It was closed.

It was 720am, remember?

But the Irish were having none of that for the poor Americans coming home from a war.

They immediately found someone to tend the bar and started serving up pints of beer. Our new mission was to see how many pints of Guinness we could consume before we took our next flight in two hours. It was my first time in Ireland, and it left a great impression on me.

Several pints and two hours later, a well-intoxicated group made their way back onto the plane. The plane bathroom was about to get a workout.

Our next stop after flying for five hours and thirty minutes was Bangor, Maine, but it was only 915am local time.

This was one of the most fun, crazy and exciting days of my life.

As we stepped into the terminal for our ninety minute layover, we were met by hundreds of people.

At first, I didn't realize they were there for us, but soon it became apparent that they were there to welcome the troops home. Us! We were the "troops".

Wow!

They had a full marching band playing music.

The VFW was there in full uniform, saluting us and shaking our hands. People were cheering for us like we had just won the Super Bowl, the World Series, and World Cup all at once.

They were hugging us and slapping us on the back, telling us "thank you" over and over. Kids were actually asking us for our autographs. It was one of the most unreal things I have ever experienced. This went on the entire time we were there.

I've got to admit, I had to wipe away a tear now and then. I wish everyone could experience this once in their lives.

At this point, we are up to over seventeen hours of travel time so far. This does not make for a happy traveler, but we were motivated.

We were in the USA now, and on our way to people we knew.

We tried to stay focused.

Fox had called Eaker to try to set up the rest of our trips, but we quickly found out there were some problems. The people in "travel" at Eaker had only set us up to get as far as our next flight. After that, we would have to call them each time we needed another flight, and book them one at a time. For whatever reason, our next flight took us to Seymour Johnson Air Force Base in North Carolina.

Why weren't we flying directly to Eaker AFB I had no idea.

It was simple in my head, but apparently, life wasn't as easy as my brain told me it should be.

When Fox tried to call the travel office to get the next flight from North Carolina to Arkansas, we discovered the time change meant they weren't even open yet. Our only solution was to wait until we arrived in North Carolina. Frustration started to rear its ugly head among the tired troops.

We boarded our plane again and headed to North Carolina. It was a short flight, and by now we had lost our sense of humor.

Crappy food, tired and severely jet-lagged, we got off the flight and made our way to a phone to call Eaker. The "travel" people there were clueless. They couldn't find us flights home from there for at least twenty-four or more hours, but told us to keep calling them back to see what they could come up with. Remember, this was before cell phones and the internet.

We couldn't just look this stuff up for ourselves.

I had made enough flight reservations for myself in the past that I knew this was a load of crap and I could do better. I started making calls to all of the different airlines for myself.

After several hours of the travel office being useless, I found a flight from Raleigh, North Carolina to Nashville that left about 8pm, but we weren't in Raleigh, we were sixty-five miles away. We called the travel office at Eaker and told them we wanted the flight from Raleigh to Nashville. They asked what we would do after that, and we told them we would figure it out for ourselves.

We survived a fucking war, we sure as hell could figure out how to get our asses from point A to point B in the United States.

We found a person in the travel office at Seymour Johnson and told them our problem. People seemed to be very sympathetic to the troops coming home, and they quickly arranged a bus to take us from the base to the airport in Raleigh.

Ninety minutes later, with our M-16 rifles in hand, we piled out of a bus and into the airport in Raleigh.

Stop for a second and picture this.

Nine guys who were bleary-eyed and travel weary, falling out of a bus and into a civilian airport terminal, each carrying M-16s and our duffel bags. We had been carrying these fucking guns for so long now, we didn't give them a second thought.

Even pre-911, we looked mighty suspicious.

Airport security immediately found us.

We quickly explained our situation, and believe it or not they allowed us to continue carrying our rifles. Maybe it helped that we didn't have any magazines in the guns.

Can you imagine the looks we were getting from the other people in the airport? At least we were in uniform and *looked* like we should be carrying these things. We went to the ticket counter to check our duffel bags and get our boarding passes. With just forty minutes until the plane took off, we barely made it to the airport. We hustled through the airport to our gate and straight to the gate agent. The look on her face when she saw us coming was priceless.

You would think that she had never seen nine guys with machine guns over their shoulders walking towards her before.

We stopped in front of her and held out our passes.

"You can *not* board this plane with those guns", she said rather forcefully.

"Ma'am, we've traveled on several planes from Saudi Arabia with these rifles, and not had a problem yet," I stammered out before Fox could get three brain cells to work together.

"Well, this isn't a military aircraft. This is a commercial aircraft with passengers. We don't allow any firearms in the cabin."

"Ma'am," I said, as sympathetically as I could muster, "we don't even have bullets for these things."

But by the look on her face, she wasn't going to budge on this.

"Okay," I said before she could deny us again, "Tell us what we can do to get on that plane. We're just trying to get home."

"Hold on, let me make a call," she said.

She picked up the phone and spoke to someone higher in the chain than her. "Okay," she said, "We can check the guns and give them back to you at the end of the flight."

I looked at Fox as he wrestled with that decision. We were all looking at him, daring him to say "no".

I didn't care if they took these fucking rifles and threw them out the window. Getting home was job one right now.

Finally, he said "okay" and we had an airport security person collect them and put them somewhere.

Who cared? We were getting on that plane!

A few minutes later, we sat back and relaxed for our ninety minute flight to Nashville, Tennessee. I actually felt like I was in my home territory. I had been to Nashville a few times, so although I didn't know the town well, at least I had been there, and for me, that was close enough. I could realistically rent a car and drive back from there, so I wasn't as antsy anymore, but I still wanted to finish this fiasco. As soon as we made it to Nashville, we had forty minutes to catch a connecting flight to Memphis and from Memphis a bus was being sent to drive us to Eaker.

We quickly collected our bags and guns and made our way to the next gate. This time, before the agent could even start the conversation, we quickly told her what the last plane did for us, so she could just do the same thing. She made a call anyhow, and ended up checking our guns just like the last lady did.

We sat on our last plane, finally.

Ninety more minutes later, we were in Memphis, which was the nearest, largest town with an airport to Eaker AFB. In my mind, I felt like they should have sent a plane for us, but I hear buses are much cheaper. We found our bags and guns one more time and loaded our asses into the bus. It was 11pm local time. We had been moving forward for over twenty-four hours now.

The bus met us outside. It wasn't until we shoved our bags on the bus, sat down and the bus started to pull away that I felt like I could actually take a deep breath and feel like I was done.

Done jumping from plane to bus to plane.

Done trying to convince travel agents, and military travel people and everyone in between that we needed to be somewhere to go somewhere to catch something.

It felt nonstop.

Now my brain had a chance to stop thinking ahead. We were on our way to our destination. Twenty-four hours ago, I was knocking sand off of my boots in Saudi Arabia, boarding a plane from a war. It had only taken six plane rides and three buses but we were finally on our way home.

Well, almost home.

I still had to make it back to Kentucky, back to *my* people.

Chapter 80
Welcome Home

At 1:30am, our bus of tired-ass firemen finally rolled through the gate of Eaker AFB and up to the fire department. There were actually people there to meet us and clap for us when we stepped off the bus. Most of them were the families of the guys who were married. The guys who were on shift at the fire department were there too, as well as the chief and assistant chief.

As much as I appreciated everyone who was there, it was anticlimactic for me. I didn't have any family here, so my homecoming was yet to come.
Sgt. Pennington gathered us all into the truck bay of the fire department with our bags.

"As of tomorrow, you are all officially on leave, and can take up to thirty days. After that, you will come back and resume your regular duties. There are reserve personnel currently here who will eventually rotate out and back to their own bases. We will have you sign paperwork for leave tomorrow morning, and then you are free to take as much of those thirty days as you like. Welcome home."
And with that, we were free to leave. Drew was there to drive me back to our dorm room.

I didn't know how the other guys felt, but I was a bit disoriented.

To go from one extreme environment to another so quickly was messing with my brain. No desert heat or people wearing odd clothes. No beer or wine to brew. No roof to party on tomorrow. All of the friends I had made over the last several months were gone. The air even felt different. Not bad, but different.

I was exhausted. We threw my bag into Drew's car and headed back to the dorm. Once inside the room, it was bleak. My mom and step-dad had been there and had removed most of my stuff. It didn't feel like my place anymore. Nowhere felt like "my place" anymore.

I was too tired to care much. I just wanted to collapse and sleep. I told Drew I'd fill him in on the clusterfuck of a travel day I'd just had tomorrow. With my bag thrown in a corner, I took off my uniform that still had desert sand embedded into the fabric, and fell into my own bed.

I was instantly asleep.

In the United States of America.

Finally.

Chapter 81
Kentucky

I woke up in Arkansas for the first time in eight months. I just lay in bed for a few minutes to get my bearings. Everything had changed, and it was going to take a bit to get my head wrapped around all of this. I had to switch gears now and try to put my life back on the train track that got derailed last year.

But it really didn't get derailed. It had just changed directions.

Eight months ago, I was just about to leave the Air Force and start my last two semesters of college. I was also engaged to a girl who spent most of her time pissing me off. Now I had no idea how long it would be until the military let me leave its clutches, and I had a new and wonderful girl in my life. But first, I had to sign some papers and get the hell out of Arkansas. Kentucky was waiting for me, and the sooner I had the bluegrass under my feet, the better.

I didn't have a car. This was making traveling home a bit more of a challenge, but if nothing else, my clusterfuck of a trip home from Saudi had made me a guru of making fast travel arrangements on the fly. After a quick shower, I called Delta and made the first flight reservation out of Memphis they had for later in the afternoon. I told Drew to get his lazy ass out of bed. He was going to have to be my chauffeur today. That paperwork for leave wasn't going to sign itself. He drove me to the fire department so I could officially go home.

As I walked inside, I was met by faces I didn't recognize.

When the ten of us left for Saudi, we were replaced by Air Force Reserve guys. For the last eight months, they had moved in and taken over our jobs. I felt like a stranger walking around my own house and not knowing who was who.

Great, just one more thing to mess with my head. "Who cares?" I thought. I'm leaving and will deal with this later.

I found Sgt. Laugh A Lot Pennington in his office and knocked.

"Come in," he said.

"I came in to sign my paperwork for leave," was all I said.

We had zero personal communication, so I just wanted to make this quick and painless.

I *really* wanted to make some comment about how disappointed he must be that none of us died, but that was a can of worms that I didn't need to open, at least right now.

I was on "mission get the hell out of Arkansas and back to Kentucky as fast as humanly possible" and sparring with Pennington felt counterproductive to my mission. He already had the paperwork on his desk, so I signed on the appropriate lines.

He asked, "How much leave do you intend to take, Sgt. White?"

"I'll probably take all thirty days," I said.

"If you intend to come back earlier, let us know so we can put you on the schedule," was all that he could add.

Fine with me.

I thought it was odd that he didn't want to know anything about my last eight months, but at the same time, he had never asked me a personal question since I'd arrived here, so why change now? I left his office and found Drew.

He drove me back to our room so I could pack a bag to go home. I opened my duffel bag and dumped the contents on the floor.

I just looked at it for a moment.

This was all of the stuff that I had used for the last eight months to work in, party in, travel in and live in.

I picked up a shirt.

It felt weird now.

The detergent and the water in Saudi had made all of my clothes feel stiff and dry. Over there, it all felt normal, but now it felt odd. Did I look that way to people back home? Did Saudi do that to me as well? I certainly *felt* different. Hopefully, this would pass soon.

I grabbed a normal suitcase and started throwing clean clothes for home into it. There really wasn't much left in my closet and drawers, so my options were limited. I didn't care. Whatever I needed, I'd buy when I got home.

I called my mom. She needed to know my flight information so she could pick me up at the airport. One more fucking plane ride, ugh.

"Hi, Mom. I got home late last night," I said. "I just booked a flight home from Memphis." I gave her my information and told her I'd see her later today. I had called her a couple of times the night before to let her know I had made it into the United States, so she had an idea I'd be home soon. I didn't want to surprise her too much. She needed to be kept in the loop.

Soon we were back in Drew's car and heading south to Memphis. I was able to tell Drew about the time in Saudi as he drove. That's when I got the first inkling that trying to explain what happened to anyone who wasn't there didn't work very well. It was like describing the color red to a colorblind person. He just nodded and listened, but how to do you tell someone about almost being killed, or feeling a 120-degree day, or any of the things most people don't usually experience?

I later came to realize that no matter how many times I told people about the things that we experienced, they really couldn't grasp the full measure of what we went through. At first, it came with a level of frustration as a person's eyes would just kind of glaze over. Later, I just came to accept it. I began to talk less about it with people on the outside and gravitate closer to people who could relate on some level. But all of that would come later.

Once in Memphis, Drew dropped me off at the airport, and I made my way to the gate after dropping off my bag. I was getting tired of airports, but I knew this one would be the best, so I sucked it up and tried to chill out. This was giving me a chance to blend back into a civilian lifestyle. None of these people had any idea where I had just been, or what I had been doing. I was trying to enjoy just being a normal everyday American, on their way to somewhere else. I wasn't sure if I was pulling it off or not, but no one was looking at me strangely, so that was a plus.

Four hours and one layover later, I was walking off the plane in my own airport, in my own state. Finally.

It was stupid, but I took a deep breath of air.

Kentucky air.

I had made it.

Back from a war and the end of a crazy-ass journey.

Would I seem different to the people I knew and loved? Would they understand how I felt now? As little as I went through for being in a war, I began to understand why some of the vets from previous wars felt like outcasts and had a hard time being home again. I only had a small taste of real war, and now I felt out of place. I hoped this was only temporary and I'd eventually feel normal again, whatever normal was now. I walked towards baggage claim, wondering where I would meet my mom.

It had only been a few hours since I told Mom I was coming home, but in that small amount of time, she had rallied the troops. As I approached baggage claim, I began to hear cheering and yelling and whooping. I wondered what all of the commotion was about, but then I saw the people making all of the noise were my friends and family.

Cousins, aunts, uncles, my mom, and friends.

They were holding signs up welcoming me home.

It took some great effort not to burst into tears.

I tried to hug everyone all at once.

It was a hero's welcome, but I didn't feel like a hero.

I had done nothing heroic at all. I had been forced to go to a war, did what I absolutely had to do while I was there, partied my ass off, fell in love, and came home the second I could. I felt like I didn't deserve any of this, but they were happy to see me, and I was happy to see them.

There were even some Vietnam vets there saluting my return. I didn't know if they were just there every day, waiting for people to return, or had heard another guy was coming home, but it was a grand gesture.

I thanked them each.

We collected my bag and headed home. Apparently, there was a party to attend in my honor.

Chapter 82
Outside Looking In

Every road we turned on and every street we took to get home was a treat. I had tried to remember all of this at one time or another while I was gone. Streets, houses, restaurants, all of the places and things and people from home. Sometimes I had worried I would forget some of this and it would become a blurred memory. Luckily, I wasn't gone so long that I forgot, but I understood how that could happen. It felt good to be home, but part of me felt like a stranger.

I wanted to shake this feeling, and hoped with a little time it would pass. I just needed to relax and not let this worry me. Not yet at least. My feet had just hit the ground, so I told myself to go with the flow and get my bearings. Man, I could use a beer, or some SID.

We turned on to my street and I looked up at the sign, "Center Park Drive." Home.

The street I grew up on, where I rode my skateboard and bike.

The street where I walked to my friends' houses and played hide-and-go-seek.

Everything looked the same.

It was me who was different.

Fuck.

I had to chill the hell out and stop mentally freaking out. I was usually a pretty even-keeled and relaxed guy, but the feelings I was having didn't belong to the old me. Maybe a few drinks would help. Right? Oh, great, now I'm an alcoholic. Who cares? One problem at a time.

The car pulled into the driveway. I was home.

This was as "home" as "home" got.

There stood the house I grew up in.

Fuck, man!

If being in there didn't reset my brain, nothing would.

We got out of the car and I grabbed my bag. Honest to God, I wanted to drop and kiss the driveway, but I somehow refrained. I just stood there looking at this building and taking it all in. I had tried so hard for so long to get back to this place, it somehow didn't seem real or possible that I had actually made it. If my outer self looked like what I was feeling on the inside, I'm not sure what my mom and stepdad would have done. Best just to grab my shit and go inside.

We opened the door and my friends and family were already there. Banners were hung saying "WELCOME HOME". It was amazing they were able to gather all these people and all this stuff in the short amount of time since I had told my mom I was coming home.

I hugged everyone. I wasn't much of hugger before, but somehow I just turned into one. It felt good. *They* felt good.

But each time I looked at someone, I felt like they were looking back at me to see if it was really me, as if I had been swapped by some crazy war replacement me.

Was Jim still in there?

Man, I hoped so.

Someone put a beer in my hand, and I was only too glad to gulp it down. Yep, that helped. Yep, that was a bad sign. Whatever.

After making the rounds and making sure I saw everyone, I tried to tell a couple of stories about my adventure. Just like with Drew, I could see that glazed look on their faces, but even more so. They didn't get it and never would. After the second story, I just stopped.

Maybe I'd tell stuff later to individuals, but most of them were just being polite.

I needed to get this stuff out of me, but this wasn't the time or the place, and these weren't the people.

It made me a little sad that my friends who I grew up with and my family were not the people to hear me spill my guts.

Fine. Fine for now at least.

I tried to turn on the "old Jim" and be the guy they remembered.
felt like a fraud.

Time. "Give yourself time," I thought.

"Where were Cowboy, Dunc, Arch and Puddin?" I wondered.

What was going on back at "the roof"?

I was certainly a bit mixed up. But hold on, it gets better, I
promise. Remember? It's a love story.

Chapter 83
Jersey Girl

It wasn't long after I arrived home that I called Mary. She was back in New Jersey and I was itching to see her. I figured being home for a week would be nice but then I'd be zipping off to the Garden State.

A couple of days after arriving home, I had a very uncomfortable meeting with Martha. I wanted to pull the rest of this band-aid off, so I had gone to her house and asked for the engagement ring back.

She only punched me once, so that was nice.

Now I officially never had to see her again. Chapter closed. Book finished. Time to move on.

I told mom my plan. I was going to New Jersey to ask Mary to get married. She was so excited I'd broken things off with Martha, she actually suggested where I could have the new engagement ring made. She used a guy to make all of her jewelry and gave me his phone number. I immediately called him to get this project moving.

There wasn't much time.

After a lengthy conversation about how it should look, he gave me some bad news. He couldn't get it to me until the day after I planned on being in New Jersey.

Crap.

He gave me an alternative. What if he shipped it to Mary's house? Hmmmmm.

Okay, I hatched an elaborate plan in my devious mind. I would go to New Jersey, then tell Mary I had forgotten my wallet and was having it shipped overnight to her house. Sneaky, right? I gave the jeweler Mary's home address and the plan was set.

A couple of days later, I was on another airplane. Mary picked me up at the airport and drove me to her house. Time to meet the parents. Mary's mom and dad are from Ireland, so this was going to be an interesting day.

I already had a warm place in my heart for Ireland since they opened their pub for us at the airport a few days ago, so maybe this meeting would go just as nice.

How would I feel about a guy coming to my house who met my daughter during a war? I hoped to make a good impression.

Her mother welcomed me with open arms. Apparently, she didn't care for Mary's last boyfriend/fiance, so I already had a slight leg up. Also, she had apparently talked me up a bit, so maybe I didn't have to try so hard. Her dad was warm, but I could tell he wasn't going to invest very much into me just yet.

I couldn't blame him.

I wondered how he was going to react after I slid that ring on his daughter's finger.

Time would tell.

Mary had made plans of her own. We would hang around her house for a couple of days, then take a little get-away trip to Cape May. It was a seaside town in southern New Jersey. Sounded good to me.

She had contacted a bed and breakfast and made reservations. We had dinner that night, then eventually off to our separate bedrooms.

No shacking up at mom and dad's house. That was fine.

The next morning the doorbell rang. UPS was there to deliver my package. Perfect. I signed for the package and acted relieved to finally have my wallet. I opened it in private and removed the ring box. I opened the box to get a look. Wow! This was perfect!

I wasn't exactly an expert in diamond rings, but this one looked like it belonged on Mary's finger. I shoved it in my jacket pocket and decided I'd find the right time in Cape May to pop the question. My palms were already a little sweaty.

Before our little excursion south, Mary took me to New York City for my first time. The Big 'ole freaking Apple. I had always wanted to see it and was glad she was the one showing it to me.

We did all of the tourist things.

Times Square.

Statue of Liberty.

Even the observation deck of the Twin Towers of the World Trade Center.

It was exciting.

What a long road this had been. Less than a year ago I was locked into a crappy relationship and it took a war to save me. Now I was with a great girl in the coolest city in the world. Things were looking up.

My first impression of New Jersey wasn't good. Flying into Newark Airport isn't a pretty sight. It's very industrial looking. Not a speck of the "Garden" part of the state. The city Mary grew up in, Bergenfield, looked like a nice, typical city, so it wasn't all doom and gloom.

On our way to Cape May, we made a pit stop. We stopped at McGuire AFB to see our friends, Dee and Renate. They had come back and resumed their lives in New Jersey, being reservists. We got a hotel room and invited them over and commenced to have a rooftop inspired, get-together fest. It was so good to see them again. Being around others from the war was easier than being around most everyone else.

Maybe it was a crutch, but for now, it was what I needed and it was good to see old/new friends.

The next day, we headed out to Cape May.

This was a quiet, resort town with large painted-ladies bed and breakfasts. The one Mary had picked for us was part B&B and part museum. The lady who ran the place was a sweet woman who cooked so well she had published a cookbook, so we were set.

Awesome town, awesome place, awesome girl.

Now I just had to figure out exactly how I was going to pop the question.

We walked around the beach area for a few hours. There were pieces of shipwrecks strewn along the shore. It was cold and the wind was blowing. A very harrowing and dramatic place. We wandered around, holding hands, wondering what might have happened in this place that put these ghostly hulks here.

All the day, I had been increasingly nervous. I wanted to get this ring out of my pocket, but I wanted it to be the "right time".

Now?

Now?

Here?

Now?

When we got back to the B&B I looked around the large living room. It seemed more like a movie set. Bright colors, comfy furniture, winding staircase, knick-knacks from a different century. *This* looked like the perfect spot. We went to the room to clean up a bit, then I told her I was going downstairs and to meet me there when she was done. I wondered if she knew what I was up to.

I paced around the room, waiting for her to come down. Finally, she came down the staircase.

My heart was beating like a rabbit, and my palms were dripping. I felt as panicked as my first S.C.U.D. attack.

She just looked at me and I could tell she knew *something* was up. I told her to sit down in one of the big, overstuffed chairs.

When she did, I pulled out the ring, got down on one knee and said the words. Holy crap! (To clarify, I actually said, "Will you marry me?" Not "holy crap" while shoving a ring in her face.)

My heart was about to pound out of my chest!

She smiled big, and said "YES!" as she hugged me.

She told me I had been acting odd all day, and now she finally understood why. Mission accomplished! Whew!

Epilogue
Deja Vu

Southbound on I-75, heading towards Florida. I'd made this trip plenty of times in the last twenty-seven years since that fateful day back in 1990. Gone were the banners hanging from the overpasses. Gone was the speedy, little, rocket car and the crazy fiancée. It was a hot, June day, and as I looked ahead, I could see the heat coming off the pavement of the highway, shimmering in the sun, making the road look like a desert mirage. Suddenly I was reminded of the day after leaving Eaker AFB for the last time. My first day as a civilian in nearly five years.

I was flying down the highway. Westbound. Dunc and Puddin where behind me. Somewhere.

I had signed my official "release" papers from the Air Force that morning. It had taken almost five months since we arrived back home before the military would let me go. Five months of dicking around Eaker AFB, being in limbo. They knew I was about to get out so they didn't give me any extra duties, or put me in charge of anything. I was just there.

In Saudi, I had been the crew chief of the rescue team, but now I wasn't allowed to even get near that truck. I had been put on different fire trucks as the driver, or the lineman, but no more being in charge of anything for me. It was a frustrating feeling to go from being in charge of so much, and having so much responsibility, to absolutely zero. I really couldn't blame them.

Why put any time or effort into someone who's about to walk out the door?
I just bit my lip and waited until they let me go. With two weeks before the fall semester of college slated to begin, they finally let me out.

When we got back to the States, Dunc discovered that his best friend, let's call him Martin, had shacked up with his wife.

Somehow, the three of them were able to work things out and there were no hard feelings.

I was amazed.

In fact, things were so good that when Dunc needed a car to drive to the other side of Arkansas to see Cowboy on the day I got out of the Air Force, his "ex" best friend let him borrow his Monte Carlo. Our friend, karma, came along for the ride as well.

We started out early. My car was completely loaded down and packed solid with the rest of the stuff from my dorm room that my mom hadn't taken months earlier. Dunc and Puddin had picked up two cases of beer to keep them lubricated during the trip to see Cowboy. It was my last big party/trip to exit the military and start college in a few days. Seeing Cowboy would be the best way to do that. It would be a nice bookend to this entire journey.

For the last few hours, I had been following the Monte Carlo, watching empty beer cans flying out the window at regular intervals. After about three hours, and what must have been a case of beer, I decided to get a little ahead of them, so I put the pedal down and zoomed ahead. A few turns and hills in the road later, I no longer saw them in my rearview mirror.

What I *did* see was a long plume of black smoke snaking into the clear blue sky. Hmmmmm.

I decided to pull over and wait for them to catch up. A couple of minutes later, no Monte Carlo.

Uh oh.

I did a U-turn through the median and hauled ass eastbound, and as I got closer to the black smoke I could barely believe my eyes.

The car was on fire. Completely engulfed in flames.

Dunc and Puddin were beside the car, shirts off, trying to grab stuff out of the inferno.

I did what anyone else would have done. I grabbed my video camera and started recording.

I did another U-turn and parked well behind the flaming car. As I ran up to them with the camera rolling, they were using their shirts to start beating at the grass beside the car, because it had caught on fire too. The car was on fire, the grass was on fire, and all the stuff they had thrown out the car and into the grass started to catch fire, too.

It was hilarious!

They were so drunk, staggering around, yelling at each other and trying to slow the unstoppable flames. I couldn't stop laughing as I conducted the interview on what had happened since I passed them. Dunc was trying to give a blow-by-blow explanation of the event as flames still spread behind him, and Puddin kept interrupting him with his personal views and commentary. I was about to pee my shorts, this was so funny.

A few minutes later, the fire department showed up.

And so did the police.

Can you close your eyes for a second and picture this?

Car on fire, practically down to its bare metal and wheels.

Grass on fire.

Smoke billowing everywhere.

Two wildly drunk guys with no shirts on staggering around and another guy with a video camera in his hand.

Fire truck.

Police cars.

There are so many different ways this could go from here. Dunc is trying to bond with the firemen, explaining that he is also a fireman. They really don't care. They just want to put the fire out before Dunc's breath causes further damage.

He keeps yelling about how he's a hero and saved babies and luggage and maybe world peace.

Puddin keeps calling Dunc a liar and continues to make fun of him.

The police are standing back, wondering what the hell to do with everyone.

Technically, no one saw the heavily intoxicated guys driving, so no reason to arrest them for DUI. Sure, they were super drunk, but they weren't really hurting anyone out here on the side of the highway, and arrests were loads of paperwork anyhow. Also, they gathered we had all just got back from Saudi Arabia, and it was still fresh enough that being in the war had some meaning, so let's not arrest nice, drunk, war-dudes.

The officer asked me if I could drive them the rest of the way to our destination. I showed him that my car didn't have ten inches of free space in it. Eventually, he decided it would just be easiest for everyone if he gave the guys a ride to the first exit he could find.

Oh boy, did he just make a crazy decision.

The guys piled into the back of the police car with the few possessions that hadn't burst into flames. I'm sure the next ten minutes of this trooper's life were ones he never forgot. I followed them off the next exit and to a little store on the side of the road, in the middle of nowhere. Sure enough, they got out, no handcuffs, and thanked the officer.

We found a pay phone to call Cowboy and explain our situation to him. We were still two hours from his house, so it would be a long while until he could come pick up the guys. With little left to do, we went inside the store to harass the poor woman behind the counter.

Dunc recounted the entire story to the woman, leaving no detail untold. In fact, he may have repeated himself several times. When he came to the end, the woman said there was a place behind the store with some chairs to wait for Cowboy. With a few hours to kill, we bought some more beer and went out back to have a party.

I kept the camera going during some of this next part. The guys didn't slow down a lick with the beer, and I had to join in as well. Dunc kept telling the story over and over and over, making it more graphic and heroic each time. Puddin kept making fun of him and pissing him off, which became more and more hilarious.

You can drink a lot of beer in two hours.

People were falling down by the time Cowboy arrived.

He saw the condition everyone was in and just laughed. I had refrained somewhat on my own beer drinking, knowing I had to drive two hours still. The poor lady at the store was ready for us to go, since we had been causing quite a commotion behind her store for the last few hours. The guys piled into Cow's car and off we went.

More beer cans flew out of Cowboy's car for the next few hours. Somehow, we made it to his house without anything else catching on fire or police showing up.

Minor miracle.

We had a little dinner and headed out to a secluded field in the middle of nowhere. We had been planning a special ceremony for months and it was time to get it done.

This would be the final chapter of the war.

We had used the same rescue radio for months in Saudi Arabia. We played it on the roof. We played it at our revetment. Now that we were home, it was time to give it a *send-off.*

We turned the music on, poured gasoline over it, and lit it on fire. Under a clear, star-filled night, we just watched it burn, remembering our fires in the wheelbarrow back in the sand box.

No one spoke for a few minutes, each of us lost in our own memories.

We drank several toasts, did a few other things that I still can't write about due to legal reasons, and when the fire finally died, we got back in Cowboy's truck and slowly drove away.

The haze of memory clearing, I turned to my right and looked at Mary. She was holding my hand and smiled at me. I smiled back. We were two lucky people, and we knew it. The war didn't turn out so well for a lot of the people we knew, but we had somehow weathered our storms and made it out the other side. I looked in the rearview mirror and there was the proof.

Erin, my beautiful daughter, was just starting her third year in the Air Force. She was already twice the world traveler I was, and her future was full of grand adventures just waiting to be experienced. I was proud of her, and a bit envious as well.

She and her brother, Conor, were giggling about something. I didn't even want to know. At fourteen years old, he was as tall as I was, and showed no signs of slowing down. He had heard his parents' stories of the Air Force, and had seen how Erin was doing, and had decided that he would eventually join as well. Yup, I was one lucky guy.

When we returned from our vacation, I decided I needed to finally get this story down. I had tried a few times before, but each time was a struggle. For some strange reason, when I tried this time, the words just started flowing. It was as if the words were just waiting for me to type them. The downside to waiting so long was forgetting some of the details. Luckily, I was still in contact with a few of my friends from the war who steered me along when I got a bit lost. Most of all, Mary was able to fill in some of the holes in my memory when things got cloudy.

For as many people who were in the war, there must be a endless great stories waiting to be told. But this story is mine. How I became caught up in this great adventure, and how I made it out. I was able to say in contact with some of the guys over the years.

Tom.

Cowboy.

Puddin.

Drew.

Facebook was a big help in finding people and keeping in touch. On the other hand, some people have eluded me, no matter how hard I've tried to track them down.

I think Dunc must have gone deep undercover with the NSA.

Jonesy is probably running a string of strip clubs in Vegas.

Where everyone else ended up, I have no idea.

In the end, I wish them all the best life has to offer.

I hope you enjoyed reading my journey. The entire time I was there, I kept thinking that no one would honestly believe the crazy shit we were doing. It was better than most movies I had seen or books I had read. We kept trying to push the limits of fun, danger, excitement, and stupidity at every turn. I think we did a pretty good job. I've tried to keep that same sense of adventure alive all these years, but in completely different ways.

That's a different book though.

It's never, THE END. ATLANTIS!

Thank You

Thank you for making it this far. This is my first book, and by all accounts, I'm really not sure if anyone will read it beyond people who might know me. For my friends and family, it gives a glimpse of who I was many years ago. It certainly shaped me into the person I am today. For the rest of you, I hope it gave you a little peek into the crazy shit that happens during a war. I have to think that there must be thousands of stories like these for every war. I'm glad I was finally able to put mine down.

Special THANK YOU to Mary for not only living through this with me once, but then enduring the year it took me to dribble this out and eventually make it into a real book.

Julie must have read this at least as many times as I did in order to edit it. My first draft was pretty rough, but she eventually whipped me into shape and made this look more like a book, and less like a high school report. I have a special bottle of ChanWhitelyDunk with your name on it!

Karen, you took my crazy idea for a cover and turned it into an actual photograph. Edit, Edit, Edit, PRESTO! I'm so glad you didn't fall off that ladder!

Cowboy, Gina, Puddin and Ann. I pushed out a chapter a week to you for months to test this thing out, and you stuck it out to the end. I hope it did the truth justice.

Atlantis.